Managing Without Supervising: Creating An Organization-Wide Performance System

William B. Abernathy, Ph.D.

Copyright © 2000 by William B. Abernathy
All Rights Reserved PerfSys Press
No part of this book may be reproduced, stored in a retrieval system, or transmitted in any form or by any means, electronic or mechanical, including photocopying, recording, or otherwise without permission in writing from the Publisher.

665 Oakleaf Office Lane
Memphis, TN 38117
(901) 763-2122
www.abernathyassociates.com

Printed in the United States of America

Foreword

This book summarizes my twenty years experience working with organizations to design and manage performance systems. The concepts and strategies presented evolved with each new project.

My first design efforts involved working with a manager or supervisor to pinpoint a performance improvement opportunity. I then developed a performance measure, collected baseline data, and implemented an improvement plan. Most plans simply provided frequent feedback to employees in combination with manager recognition. Typically, an improvement in the targeted behavior was achieved.

First, much like pushing on a balloon, an improvement in the target behavior produced an adverse effect in other necessary behaviors. Second, because the target behavior was usually a problem area for the manager, it often had only a minimal impact on key organizational results. Third, I found that feedback and social reinforcers were sufficient to improve a performance – but not to sustain the improvement.

The solution to the first issue was to move to multi-dimensional measures that 'balanced' performances to produce an optimal, overall outcome. The performance scorecard serves this purpose and will be discussed in detail.

The solution to the second issue was to move toward strategically defined measures rather than measures aimed only at problem areas. Put simply, a large improvement in an unimportant measure is less valuable than a small improvement in an important one. The scorecard design approach termed the 'Method of Cascading Objectives' provided a practical vehicle for strategically defining performance measures.

The third issue's solution was to link traditional organizational reinforcers to scorecard improvement. In varying degrees, these reinforcers included incentive pay, annual performance reviews, merit increases, time-off, job assignments, and promotions.

Incentive pay proved to be the easiest of these to implement and manage. However, a truly self-sustaining performance system would need to include most of the organization's reinforcers.

These experiences have led me, as a psychologist, to appreciate—more than ever—the subtlety and complexity of human performance within an organization. It is now my belief that human behavior is best understood from a 'systems' perspective and that any meaningful and lasting changes in an organization will require this perspective and approach.

This book provides the reader this perspective as well as a number of specific systems-oriented concepts and practices. Performance systems design and management is a new and exciting field for both researchers and practitioners. I hope I have, in some small way, encouraged others to adopt and apply this perspective to both continue to expand our knowledge, and to create workplaces in which employees become true stakeholders who are committed to their organization's long-term success.

SECTION I: THE TOTAL PERFORMANCE SYSTEM

Chapter 1: A Radical Alternative to Conventional Employee Management ... 5

Chapter 2: The Seven Sins of Wages ... 20

Chapter 3: Components of the Total Performance System ... 28

SECTION II: PERFORMANCE MEASUREMENT

Chapter 4: The Evolution of the Total Performance System ... 41

Chapter 5: Case Study: Design of a Restaurant's Total Performance System ... 60

Chapter 6: The Method of Cascading Objectives ... 85

Chapter 7: The Performance Scorecard ... 98

Chapter 8: Performance Measurement Principles ... 112

Chapter 9: Performance Measurement: Sales ... 127

Chapter 10: Performance Measurement: Productivity and Expense Control ... 136

Chapter 11: Performance Measurement: Customer Service and Regulatory Compliance ... 152

Chapter 12: Performance Measurement: Project and Support Jobs ... 166

SECTION III: PERFORMANCE PAY

Chapter 13:	Alternative Pay Systems	182
Chapter 14:	Phase I: Profit-Indexed Performance Pay	188
Chapter 15:	Phase II: Stakeholder Pay	201

SECTION IV: MANAGING WITHIN A TOTAL PERFORMANCE SYSTEM

Chapter 16:	Positive Leadership	213
Chapter 17:	Performance Analysis	229
Chapter 18:	Total Performance System Administration	254
Chapter 19:	Analysis of Sixteen Organizations' Total Performance Systems	282
Chapter 20:	Managing Without Supervising	323

Chapter 1

A Radical Alternative to Conventional Employee Management

The Total Performance System is a system of employee management that significantly reduces the need for direct supervision in an organization. The most widely known application of this approach to management is at Lincoln Electric in Cleveland, Ohio, where the worker-to-supervisor ratio is an astonishing 100:1. In order to 'manage without supervising,' the organization implements a precision performance measurement system that is linked to significant incentive pay opportunities. This organization-wide performance measurement and incentive pay system is termed a 'Total Performance System' (TPS). TPS provides employees specific goals with monthly performance reporting and incentive payouts. These tools allow managers to spend much less time in direct supervision and more time planning, coordinating, and optimizing performance.

TPS developed over a period of fifteen years in a diverse group of organizations. Industry types include banking, insurance, healthcare, manufacturing, distribution, retail, and education. Employee groups range in number from 60 to over 16,000. The results obtained by these organizations are presented in Chapter 19 and referred to throughout this book. There are a number of benefits the organization accrues by implementing TPS.

A movement from 'entitlement pay' to 'performance pay.'

Traditional compensation has become an employee entitlement that is more an obstacle to an organization's success than a facilitator. Wages and salaries are fixed costs that increase over time at a compound rate. The guaranteed nature of wages and salaries restricts the earnings of employees when the company is successful, and forces layoffs when the company experiences a business downturn. Further, because pay is guaranteed, the organization typically places tight pay bands on each job position to control payroll expense. The result of this practice is a failure to equitably reward high performers (and the inverse–overpay poor performers).

Many organizations recognize the flaws in entitlement pay and are experimenting with alternative pay schemes. A recent national survey from the Hay Group finds 78% of the companies responding are implementing some sort of alternative pay system. Unfortunately, there are many potential pitfalls in designing and implementing performance pay systems. These will be addressed throughout this book.

A movement toward decentralization and outsourcing.

Over the past decade, organizations have 'downsized' their middle management ranks which increased the remaining managers' number of reports. More employees are hired on a contract, temporary or part-time basis, and the use of 'virtual employees' who work out of home offices is increasing. Mergers and acquisitions have spawned organizations whose employees are spread across the country or are multi-national.

These trends make traditional direct supervision impractical. The supervisor can no longer meet with her employees each morning and distribute work assignments. Nor can she watch employees to ensure they are on task. TPS provides the manager and supervisor with the tools they need to manage effectively in this new environment. They must learn a new approach to management that focuses on objective results, rather than subjective impressions or mere employee activity. The new manager is more a leader and facilitator than a supervisor.

A movement toward the 'nimble' organization.

Because conventional pay requires tight control over pay bands, the result has been the practice of rewarding good performers with promotions. Such promotions continuously remove high performers from their jobs. Often, these high performers have no real desire to manage, nor do they have the attributes needed to be effective managers. The practice of promoting high performers fosters multi-layer organizations with rigid hierarchies. For example, in banking it is not uncommon to see a worker-manager span of control of less than five. Such organizations find it increasingly difficult to react quickly to changes in the marketplace, competition or new technology. Further, such organizations stifle creativity and innovation due to an often-adversarial bureaucracy. TPS provides an alternative to promotions and top-heavy organizational structures, and drives decision making to the lowest possible levels of the organization.

A movement toward more concern for customers.

New competition and more demanding customers are renewing concerns about customer satisfaction and loyalty. Over the past two decades, many approaches to improving service quality have been tried. Though many of them have much to offer an organization, they often fail to produce the intended results because they are implemented in a conventional, bureaucratic organizational system. Employees often view customers as more of a nuisance or liability than an opportunity. Have you ever heard an employee comment, "Oh no, we're about to begin our busy season of the year?"

TPS re-establishes the connection between customers and employees in two ways. TPS provides timely, precise measures of service levels, customer satisfaction, and customer loyalty. TPS then shares profits with employees thereby reestablishing the connection between personal earnings and customer satisfaction. The TPS employee performs more like a self-employed person than an employee.

There are two very different schools of thought regarding the origins of employee performance. One school can be traced to our Puritan work ethic and believes that the source of employee performance is internal – it comes with the employee. In this view, there are good and bad performers, and the organization's function is to attract and retain the good ones and avoid or get rid of the bad ones. A second school of thought finds its roots in the theories of the behaviorist, B. F. Skinner. This view recognizes that employees come to the workplace with their own unique genetics, general health, and work habits. Even so, behaviorists argue that a high percentage of employee performance is influenced by the workplace itself. How the organization selects, trains, evaluates, promotes, pays, supervises, and communicates with employees has a significant impact on their performance. In fact, the argument is made that even if the organization selects employees with the right personal backgrounds, a poorly designed performance system will severely restrict their performance level.

Therapeutic vs. Systems Perspectives.

Applied Behavior Analysis (ABA) is the practical application of Skinner's behaviorism. ABA was first applied in education and later in clinical settings. These applications proved quite successful, especially with students or clients with severe behavior deficiencies or anomalies. The instructor or therapist would work one-on-one with the client often over long periods of time.

The therapeutic model is now applied to business settings and is termed 'performance management.' The supervisor became the 'therapist' and the employee the 'client.' An employee performance deficiency is pinpointed, for which the supervisor designs a performance improvement plan or 'intervention.' The results are 'charted' and the plan is adjusted if the performance change goals are not being met. To implement ABA in an organization, it is therefore necessary to provide supervisors with intensive training in performance management principles and techniques.

Though more systematic, ABA is not too dissimilar from conventional thinking about management, supervision, and leadership. Management still directs, evaluates, and controls employee behaviors. Thousands of books have been written on this topic. Often the prescription is to emulate other successful leaders from Attila and Machiavelli to today's successful military leader, business leader or sports coach. Whether we choose the *Seven Habits of Highly Successful Managers*, or prefer *One-Minute Management*, the superior-subordinate relationship is still at the core. That is, there is always a leader and one or more followers.

Over the past 20 years, some management theorists have proposed a radical alternative to the leader-follower model of management. These theories variously stress employee involvement, employee empowerment, open-book management, and self-directed teams. The benefits stated for employee empowerment were significant. They included higher employee satisfaction, higher performance, a reduction in the number of managers, improved customer service, and improved work processes, to name a few. Unfortunately, the majority of applications failed to deliver these promised benefits, and many efforts were abandoned with a resulting return to the traditional management model.

From a behaviorist perspective, these failures are not surprising. In almost every case, the traditional organizational performance system was left intact. Few adjustments were made in employee selection, training, evaluation, promotion, or pay practices. Basically, a radical departure from the leader-follower model was simply interpolated over the traditional system, a system designed to support the leader-follower model!

If the conventional hierarchical organizational structure does not support employee empowerment, what model should be used? The answer, surprisingly, is right under our noses. The alternative to centralized planning and management is, and has been, the free enterprise system. The two major strategies for organizing business interactions in societies are socialism and free enterprise. In many ways, socialism parallels the organizational hierarchical model. There are few, if any, examples of the application of free enterprise to the internal management of an organization. In the 1980s the concept of 'intrapreneurs' was introduced, but was primarily concerned with employees creating new businesses within existing businesses. Replacing conventional leader-follower relationships was not a priority.

Is it more effective to manage individual employees, or is it better to manage the behavior system in which employees work? The former is the more common view, the latter is presented here as a more desirable alternative.

Bureaucratic Management vs. Designing a Performance System.

Management is getting a group of people to do things they would not individually choose to do on a consistent basis. An audience viewing a movie does not need to be managed. People enjoying themselves in a park, or shoppers in a mall, don't need to be managed. No management is needed, because each person is pursuing his own personal interests. There is no need to direct or coordinate his efforts.

An organization's purpose, however, is to achieve common goals rather than personal ones. Some of the earliest organizations were military. The common goal was defense or conquest. Management had to persuade the individual warrior to take risks, and endure physical hardships, they would not likely accept on their own.

Many approaches to managing people have been proposed. In early years, there were tribal chiefs and kings, or oligarchies in which a tribal council or plebiscite ruled. As groups grew larger, management hierarchies were required with multiple layers of staff and line officers. Several other theories of social organization were proposed. Democracy substituted the will of the majority for the will of the leader. Thomas Moore described a society led ultimately by God's will. Plato preferred a philosopher-king. Rousseau and Thoreau opted for no management at all. Marx and Bellamy described an economic basis to social order. Adam Smith saw the free market as a means of managing interactions between individuals in a society. America's founders preferred a written constitution as the central guiding force.

In business organizations, the bureaucratic management model (borrowed from the military) became, and is, the most common means of managing large employee groups. This approach to management relies on several levels of managers that ensure a tight span of control (around seven subordinates reporting to each manager). Strategy and policy are communicated downward from executive managers, through middle managers, to supervisors, and ultimately, to the worker. Bureaucratic management is characteristically inflexible and slow to respond to changes in the marketplace. It is a relatively costly approach to management because it creates several levels of employees who do not directly produce anything.

Beginning in the 1970s, many management theorists proposed that the bureaucratic approach with its senior managers, middle managers, supervisors, and support staff could be modified or replaced by 'empowering' employees to make more decisions on their own. Decisions would be made by those closest to the work. Productivity, quality, and customer service would improve. Employee morale and commitment would improve. Self-managed teams and individuals would be able to save money by eliminating costly management levels. Unfortunately, most companies only paid lip service to the idea, and those that did implement rarely obtained the results as advertised. The missing element was a conceptual base to organize this empowerment effort. An alternative to the bureaucratic management system was missing.

A farmer harvests his crop and sells it to a granary. The granary then pays another organization to transport the crop. The crop is transported to a food processor which then sells the product to a wholesale distributor. The wholesale distributor sells his product to a grocer, who then sells it to the consumer. Who manages this complex process? It is driven by the marketplace. In each interaction, one party is a seller and the other a buyer. Their mutual, best interests coordinate each transaction. There is no leader – only a marketplace.

This free market approach to feeding our nation is amazingly effective and efficient. The consumer has a wide variety of choices at reasonable prices. Contrast this with the constant shortages experienced in countries that attempt a central planning approach to food production and distribution. The free market can be an extremely effective alternative to traditional bureaucratic management.

Can an analog to the free market be implemented within an organization? Such a system would have to measure the output of individual workers, or worker teams, who would become 'sellers' of their products. The buyers (managers, customers, and stockholders) would need the ability to directly pay the worker for her products and services. Finally, the total system would have to act as an 'economy' that would adjust prices (incentive pay opportunity) to ensure coordination and alignment among the various employee teams.

Over the past twenty years, we have experimented with all sorts of organizational analogs to the free market. The result, 'The Total Performance System' (TPS) has been successfully implemented in a wide variety of organizations. TPS defines individual and team (seller) work outputs using the performance scorecard format. The scorecard measures are directly aligned with the overall organizational strategy using the 'Method of Cascading Objectives'. Employees are directly paid for their products and services through an incentive pay system. The value of the employees' products and services (incentive pay opportunity) is indexed to the overall net income of the organization (the economy).

Obstacles to the Implementation of Performance Systems.

Despite the potential of the performance systems approach to managing an organization, it is rarely applied. The one notable exception is the Lincoln Electric Company. Lincoln Electric is a 'Fortune 500' company with some 2500 employees. The company manufactures arc-welding equipment. Mr. Lincoln founded the company over 50 years ago with a performance systems management philosophy and practice. Workers are treated as though they are self-employed. There are no wages – each employee is paid for what they produce on a piece-rate system. Employees also share directly in the profits of the company. Except for an annual plant shutdown, there are no paid vacations or sick days. Employees pay for their own health insurance.

The results are impressive. Lincoln provides its employees lifetime employment, and has not had a layoff in many years. Lincoln claims to have the highest paid factory workers in the world. Turnover is very low. The ratio of workers to managers is 100:1. Lincoln management is evangelical about its approach to management. Tours and seminars are provided to other companies at no charge. Lincoln is used as a case study at the Harvard Business School; Lincoln's approach is studied by managers and management theorists all over the world.

Lincoln has consistently demonstrated high productivity and product quality, exceptional employee commitment, and an empowered employee group that requires minimal supervision. Yet, there are few if any, actual examples of the application of the Lincoln approach in other organizations. Why is this? Given a choice, most organizations and their employees, would agree that Lincoln's approach is much superior to bureaucratic management.

There are five obstacles that must be addressed for a successful implementation of the performance systems approach to management. These obstacles include a reliance on subjective impressions, the effort required to change, a change in the locus of control, entitlement thinking, and commodity labor thinking.

Subjective Management. Very few organizations consistently gather objective performance data for individual employees or small teams. Consequently, the manager and the worker must rely on subjective impressions and exceptions (errors) to evaluate performance. Bureaucratic organizations reinforce this practice by institutionalizing subjectivity through the annual performance review process.

When we analyze and manage non-human processes such as finances or computer systems, we do so quite differently than when we manage other people. Managers don't have social interactions with equipment or mechanical processes. It is difficult for a manager to separate how they feel about a person from the person's performance. Everyone has prejudices that influence their perceptions of others. It is often difficult to distinguish the result from the person.

I was hired to help a restaurant chain increase its wine and liquor sales. When I arrived at the pilot restaurant, the first thing I did was ask the three managers to rank-order the cocktail servers in terms of their sales performances. I then compared their rankings with the actual sales of servers over the past few months. I was surprised to find that the server ranked as the worst salesperson was in fact the best – best by over fifty-percent sales per table.

On further investigation, I found that this server reacted negatively to people in authority. In fact, she included me in her dislike of management. Therefore, I began to dislike her as much as the managers. However, when she dealt with customers she was a completely different person. The managers were rating her sales performance in terms of her interactions with them, rather than her actual sales.

The adverse impact of subjective management practices is substantial. Managers and co-workers label people as good and bad performers, and these labels often stick regardless of changes in actual performance. As chronicled in *the Peter Principle* and Whyte's classic, *The Organization Man*, many employees rise through the ranks due to social skills rather than through their actual performance or organizational contribution. The socially awkward are often not recognized for the same reasons. Subjective impressions provide little direction or feedback to employees, and thus largely fail as effective performance management tools. As a result, it is rare that employees perform at a level close to their potentials.

Change Effort. Managers resist objective measurement because they personally benefit from the existing subjective management process, and objective management requires effort and change. Subjective management empowers the manager, who has discretionary control over each subordinate's organizational fate. Managers reward employees that they like, and ignore or punish those they don't like. Employees learn to become subservient to managers to gain their favor and avoid their wrath. Linking pay and recognition directly to objective performance undermines employee deference and the manager's personal power.

Managing by exception is the primary means of managing in the absence of objective measurement. Rather than recognize and reinforce incremental improvements, managers simply wait for employees to fail to meet a deadline or make errors. This approach to management is easy, natural, and it feels good. Managers do not have to apply themselves to precisely defining desired outcomes, nor do they have to provide frequent feedback. Managing exceptions is natural and familiar to the manager, because he or she experienced the same approach at home, at school, and in past and present work experiences. Managing exceptions feels good because mistakes make us angry, and punishment (criticism, sarcasm, suspension, demotion, etc.) is a natural and stress reducing response to anger.

Shifting the Locus of Control. Managers that adopt the system view can no longer easily blame employees for departmental failures. Failures to perform are first viewed as problems in the system, such as problems in selection, training, resources, equipment, staffing and scheduling, coordination, work assignment, direction, feedback, and compensation. In a well-designed performance system, these tools are all under the direct control of the manager. The manager can no longer simply sit in the office and complain about employees. This change from reactive to proactive management requires effort, learning new skills, and abandoning practices that were often personally rewarding.

I once taught a course in performance management for prison guards. After the first week, it became apparent that lectures were boring them. I decided to demonstrate the differences between positive reinforcement (incentives) and negative reinforcement (intimidation). The next week I brought two white rats and two Plexiglas boxes to class. Each Plexiglas box had a lever mounted on its side that the rat could push with its paw (see illustration).

POSITIVE REINFORCEMENT   NEGATIVE REINFORCEMENT

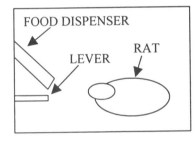 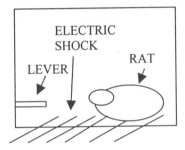

In the positive reinforcement box, the rat could feed himself by pressing the lever, which would then drop a pellet of food from the food dispenser. In the negative reinforcement box, the rat could prevent an electric shock to his feet by pressing the bar.

I began my demonstration with positive reinforcement. Since rats do not naturally press levers to feed themselves, I had to 'shape' the rat's behavior by feeding it for successive approximations to the desired behavior. I began by feeding the rat whenever he looked at the bar, then when he approached, and so forth until he actually pressed the bar and fed himself. This process required a little over a half-hour to complete.

To demonstrate negative reinforcement, I activated the electric shock grid. By chance, the rat jumped on the bar and inadvertently turned the shock off. To learn to continue to press the bar to keep the shock from coming on, took the rat less than twenty seconds of training. I then asked the guards what their conclusions were, based on these demonstrations. The unanimous response was that negative reinforcement was much faster, and also cheaper than positive reinforcement! This result was very discouraging.

During the class break, one of the guards picked up the positively reinforced rat and began playing with it. Noticing this, another guard picked up the negatively reinforced rat, who promptly bit down on this thumb and would not let go. The guard howled and tried vainly to shake the rat loose.

When we finally disengaged the rat and got everybody seated, I asked the guards what they now thought of negative reinforcement. The response was – you can get an animal or person to perform using negative reinforcement – you just don't want to be around them much!

Entitlement Thinking. Workers must change too. Pay and annual pay increases have become entitlements employees feel they are owed, regardless of their performance or contribution to the organization. Accountability has become anathema to many employees. Not only does this failure to accept responsibility undermine personal effectiveness, it undermines the effectiveness of the group as a whole – particularly top performers. Economists term this problem the "free rider effect." The top performer produces more, but receives essentially the same pay. To make the system fair, the top performer reduces performance to equal that of the average performer in the group. A Russian proverb related to equity under communism stated, "If you have one cow and your neighbor has two – kill one of his!"

Commodity Labor Thinking. The conventional compensation system surveys the local labor market to find out how much other organizations are paying for various jobs. They then match this pay to ensure they are paying competitive salaries to their employees. Labor is thus viewed as a commodity, like wheat or corn. A programmer in Topeka, Kansas has a certain regional market or commodity value and that is what she is paid.

About 15 percent of the labor pool operate under an alternative compensation system based upon performance rather than commodity value. These people are the self-employed. At the turn of the century some 85 percent of the labor pool were self-employed. How is the pay of a self-employed person determined? His pay is certainly not based on labor market surveys. It is based on personal performance and the performance of his organization (which may be only him). What is the maximum (or minimum) a self-employed person can earn? It is limited only by market demand for his services or products, competition, and performance.

To implement a performance system that truly mirrors the larger free market, ownership and management must distance themselves from conventional commodity notions of pay. Workers are more like partners, whose earnings are only limited by the organization's success and their personal performance. In exchange for this limitless earnings opportunity, the employee must share the business risks of the organization by accepting below-market pay when the business is in a downturn.

Though none of these five obstacles are insurmountable, they help to explain why few organizations have adopted the performance systems approach.

Chapter 2

The Seven Sins of Wages

The following is an excerpt from my earlier book, *The Sin of Wages*. Problems with conventional wage and salary systems and the annual performance review are described as the seven 'sins' of wages.

1. Fixed-Cost Pay. Pay has come to be viewed as an entitlement by employees. Employees believe they are not only entitled to their current pay, but also pay increases each year. This view makes the payroll effectively a fixed cost to the

Pay is guaranteed.

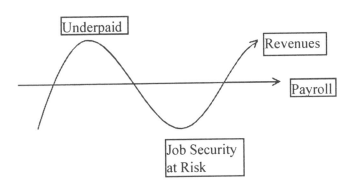

organization which grows at a compound rate due to annual pay increases. When revenues decline, profits decrease and layoffs are the only recourse. In this system, employees are risking long-term job insecurity for short-term pay guarantees.

Entitlement pay also reduces the number of people employed and the level of pay. Because pay is essentially guaranteed for life, employers are reluctant to add new employees. They are also reluctant to increase pay, when the business is successful, for fear of the high fixed expense if revenues decline. This entitlement view of pay also necessarily turns labor and management into adversaries. Management pay is often linked to profit, while the work force is artificially removed from it.

Pay increases annually.

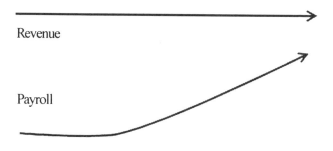

2. Pay for Time.

Employees are paid for their time.

"When you pay for time, you get time. When you pay for results, you get results." Hourly pay is particularly detrimental to employee productivity. Parkinson's law tells us "work expands to fill the time available." When you are paid by the hour, it is not in your financial interest to work more efficiently, since this will simply result in more tasks being assigned or, worse, a cutback in your hours. Employees living on overtime pay, aggravate the problem. I find it amazing that management really expects employees to form teams to develop more efficient processes, when they will simply result in their having to learn additional jobs for the same pay, or experience a cut-back in hours.

3. Corporate Socialism. Entitlement pay is unfair to good performers. It pays everyone in a given pay grade about the same regardless of their personal contribution. The result is high performance goes unrewarded and performance drifts toward mediocrity. Entitlement thinking has failed as economic policy and does not work any better inside our businesses.

Employees in the same job are paid the same.

EFFECTIVE PAY FOR 16000 UNITS

	Wage	Units /Hour	Pay /Hour	Effective Pay
HIGH PERFORMER	$8.50	100	$.085	$1,360
AVG. PERFORMER	$8.00	75	$.11	$1,760
LOW PERFORMER	$8.00	50	$.16	$2,560

The table above illustrates how conventional pay fails to adequately recognize individual employee contributions. The high performer is paid more per hour ($8.50), but also produces more than others (100 units per hour). Dividing the hourly wage by the units produced per hour, shows that the top performer is paid much less per unit produced than other performers. If the number of units produced per month was 16,000, and we multiplied the pay per hour by this number of units, we find the 'effective pay' per month of the top performers considerable less than the average or poor performer.

4. Performance-Based Promotions. Conventional pay prevents supervisors and managers from directly, and immediately, paying a subordinate for a job well done. Tight pay bands reduce the manager's ability to reward performance through annual pay increases. The consequence is that many supervisors and managers must promote top performers to reward them for their performance. This creates competition among employees and forces the best performers out of their jobs and into management. Often, top performers prefer to work

Top performers are promoted to management.

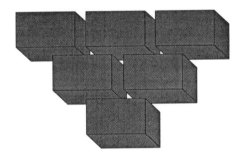

independently and do not work well through others. The result is that the company loses a good performer and creates a dissatisfied and ineffective manager.

The Peter Principle states "employees rise to the level of their incompetence." I would simply add, that the driving force behind this principle is the conventional pay system. We reward employees by promoting them until their performance no longer justifies additional promotions.

5. Management by Perception. Conventional wage and salary systems encourage and support "lazy management" practices that undermine employee effectiveness. Time-oriented pay does not require the on-going measurement of employee performance results. Because employee performance results are not measured, managers must rely on subjective perceptions to determine who is performing, and who is not. The subjective review is often invalid and delayed, and attempts to compress a year's performance in one rating.

**Management by Perception
Managers subjectively rate
employee performance once a year.**

6. *Management by Exception.* Without an objective performance measurement system, managers have no accurate means

**Management by Exception
Managers punish exceptions rather
than reward incremental improvements.**

for recognizing or rewarding improvement and must therefore manage errors. In practice, acceptable performance is largely ignored, but failures to perform are "managed." In this system, employees do not work to earn their pay, they work to avoid losing it. The results are minimum effort, absenteeism, low morale, and turnover.

7. *Entitlement Thinking.* Fifty years of guaranteed pay has created an "entitlement culture" in which employees believe they are owed their pay, regardless of personal or company performance. The technical term for pay, *compensation*, is revealing. We are compensated for going to work rather than working to *earn* a living. Entitlement thinking has created a nation of risk-averse employees who refuse accountability and are unwilling to accept the cold fact – that without a successful business, there can be no pay.

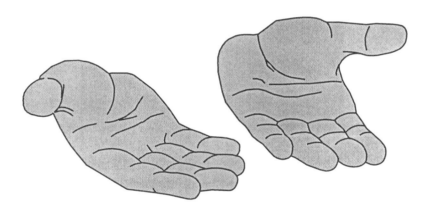

The wage and salary system became the dominant pay scheme following WWII when inflation was high and there were more jobs than people to fill them. This scheme no longer works well for most organizations and is a bad deal for the both the employee and the organization. Furthermore, the wage and salary system allows a management group to manage by perception and exception, rather than through precise performance measurement. These approaches to management have never worked very well, but are becoming an even greater liability with the continuing decentralization of organizations.

Chapter 3

Components of the Total Performance System

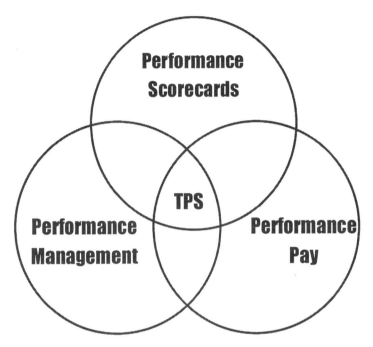

The Total Performance System (TPS) integrates three critical management components – performance scorecards, positive leadership, and profit-indexed performance pay. Although many organizations have implemented some, or even all of these components, they are rarely integrated to create a total system.

Performance Management Only. For example, an organization may train its managers and supervisors in performance management techniques, but without a formal measurement system, managers must select improvement targets on an <u>ad hoc</u> basis. As a result, improvement initiatives may not be aligned with the organization's strategy. Furthermore, without an incentive pay system, good performance management practices and continuous improvement are difficult to sustain.

Performance Pay Only. More recently, many organizations have implemented various performance pay schemes without an accompanying measurement system, or a change in conventional management practices. Examples include various bonus plan schemes that fail to define the specific performance results required to earn the incentive payment. The results of these plans are ambiguous, at best. Without formal measurement, performance pay fails to focus or reward employees for strategic outcomes. Without positive leadership training, managers restrict employee initiative and often fail to support employee improvement efforts.

Performance Measurement Only. A comprehensive performance measurement system, that drives strategic objectives down to the small team and individual employee job level, will likely improve performance. This is so even in the absence of better management practices and incentive pay (what gets measured, is what gets done). The addition of positive leadership and incentive pay to a comprehensive measurement system optimizes and sustains these results. Unfortunately, of these three components, most organizations fail to develop the measurement system while implementing management training or performance pay instead.

Why Implement a Total Performance System? An organization that does the 'right things right' will be successful. This is not news. The real question is how to accomplish this in a working organization in which everyone is struggling with day-to-day job demands. There is a vast array of literature concerning strategic planning and organizational development and change. However, much of it is descriptive rather than prescriptive. Perhaps, we need to step back from theory and abstraction and take a fresh look at an overlooked key to organizational success – the employee.

The conventional management philosophy views employees as commodities, rather than partners in the enterprise. Employees are usually unaware of the business strategy. Even if the strategy is communicated, it is rarely the case that the employee's specific role in accomplishing the strategic objectives is defined. If the strategy is to increase profitability, does the line employee know which expenses to control or which products or services are most profitable? If the strategy is to provide the highest quality service or products, does the employee know what the customer concerns are or how their performance relates to those concerns? If the strategy is to implement new technology, new products or new locations, does the employee know how he can facilitate the success of these projects?

Even if management did effectively communicate these roles, the results would still fall short. Without frequent performance feedback on key results, employees are in the dark as to how effective they are at assisting in the accomplishment of strategic objectives. Most of us know that the 'annual performance review' is a poor substitute for frequent, targeted performance information.

Finally, even if we communicated the strategy and provided effective performance feedback, we would have to ask why an employee should care if the strategy is a success or not. The line employee's pay is only indirectly related to the organization's success. Many employees have come to view pay as an entitlement which is unrelated to the organization's strategic success and profitability.

The Typical Employee

1 Does not understand the business strategy.

2 Does not know his personal role in accomplishing the strategy.

3 Does not know how well she's doing or how to improve strategic results.

4 Has no personal stake in the success of the business strategy.

Conventional management practices work, but not very well. Performance research consistently finds *employees who work under conventional management are working at about two-thirds of their capacity.* Imagine the impact on an organization if employee performances increased 33%. The effects on sales, labor cost, and service would be phenomenal. But we have become complacent in our management. Ultimately, management is the obstacle that restricts optimal employee performance.

The Result...

1 Fails to focus on the right things.

2 Does what is required, not what is needed.

3 Assumes she is performing well and does not try to improve.

4 Is not personally interested in the organization's success.

The Alternative

1. **Objective, measurable strategic objectives that are cascaded throughout the organization.**

2. **Personal or small team scorecard with specific measures and goals that drive the strategy.**

3. **Manager assistance in pinpointing improvement opportunities and designing improvement plans.**

4. **Share in the organization's success through profit-indexed performance pay.**

Components of the Total Performance System

1. Strategic Scorecard. The design and implementation of the Total Performance System begins with the creation of a strategic scorecard. The scorecard typically consists of two to seven objective measures which evaluate the progress of the organization's strategy. A base (current performance) and goal is set for each measure. Each measure is assigned a priority weight.

Sample Strategic Scorecard

Measure	Base	Goal	Weight
Controllable Net Income	$20M	$25M	40%
Working Capital Efficiency	70 days	50 days	20%
Cust. Satisfaction Survey	3.5	7.0	20%
Project Completion %	50%	90%	20%

2. **Cascading Objectives.** The strategic scorecard measures are then cascaded down through the organization to the small team and individual employee. Typically, each manager designs his or her subordinates' scorecards. This process ensures alignment with the level above, since the manager will design scorecards that drive improvement on his scorecard, which in turn drive improvements on his superior's scorecard.

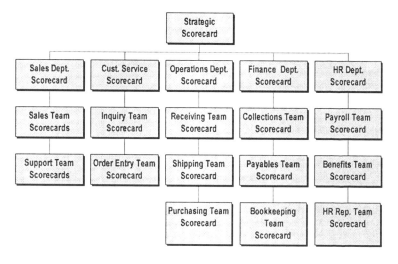

2. **Performance Scorecard.** Each month, every employee receives a performance scorecard which provides feedback on all of the team and individual measures assigned to her. The sample scorecard below is computer-generated.

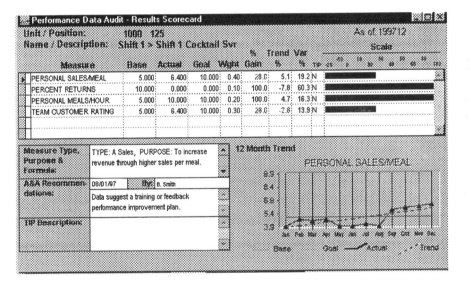

3. **Performance Charts.** In addition to the scorecard, each performance measure should be charted for the past twelve months. The performance charts help managers and workers pinpoint improvement opportunities and evaluate the effectiveness of tactical improvement plans.

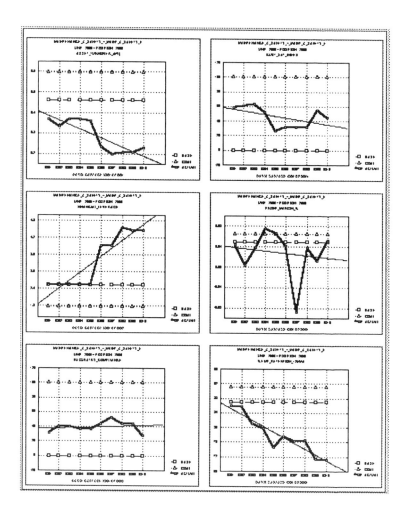

4. **Tactical Improvement Planning.** Based upon an analysis of the measure trend charts, managers and employees investigate the likely causes of the low or declining performance. This root-cause analysis is depicted in the decision tree below.

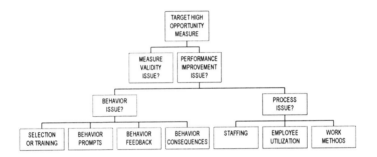

Pinpointing Obstacles to Maximum Performance

For example, an employee's job accuracy is low. We determine the measure is valid, and then must decide whether the performance deficiency is due to behavior or process issues. In discussions with the employee, we discover she is unaware of the accuracy problem. There is, then, a behavior-feedback problem. Accuracy data is provided on a daily or weekly basis and performance improves.

Positive Leadership. Managers apply positive leadership techniques to both improve performance and to create a more self-managed employee group. The effectiveness of a manager can be assessed by reviewing the average performance of her subordinates, as well as through a survey of management practices in which subordinates rate the manager's practices. The chart below illustrates how these two dimensions can be scaled on one chart.

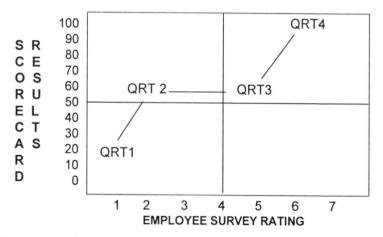

The Y-axis plots the average scorecard performance of the manager's subordinates. The X-axis plots the average of the subordinates' ratings of the manager on a 'management practices' survey. The survey is administered quarterly. Survey items deal with performance management practices that include weekly meetings, performance feedback, positive reinforcement, and other practices.

Managers who fall in the bottom left-hand quadrant are considered 'absentee managers' in that they don't effectively manage performance, nor achieve good results. Managers who fall in the bottom right-hand quadrant are considered 'paternalistic managers'. They attempt to provide employees positive reinforcement, but fail to focus on job outcomes. The upper left-hand quadrant represents the 'authoritarian' manager who gets results, but gets them through the application of negative reinforcement. The upper right-hand quadrant is the goal. This manager gets results through effective performance management practices.

System Review. Scorecard results can be converted to standard scores and aggregated to provide senior management and the system administrator with a snap shot of the Total Performance System's effectiveness.

Performance Data is Converted to Standard Scores to Provide An Executive Summary

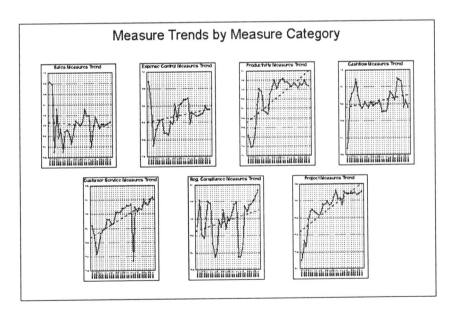

Profit-Indexed Performance Pay. All employees participate in an incentive plan in which a portion of profits are shared with employees. Each employees share is adjusted for his personal and team scorecard performance.

Profit-Indexed Performance Pay

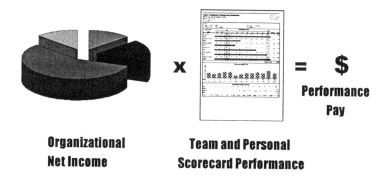

The Total Performance System is self-sustaining. Managers, and their teams, design Tactical Improvement Plans that drive improvements on tactical level scorecards. These tactical improvements, in turn, drive improvements in the strategy. As the strategy is accomplished, short- and long-term profits increase. A portion of these profit gains is shared with the employees proportionate to their scorecard improvements. This profit sharing reinforces improvement planning which then leads to new initiatives.

The Total Performance System

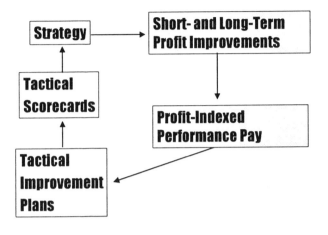

Section II: Performance Measurement

Chapter 4

The Evolution of the Total Performance System

In learning how to effectively and efficiently measure employee performance, three major issues have to be addressed. First, employee performance is multi-dimensional. How can this characteristic best be addressed by a measurement system? Second, do you measure employee activity or the results of the activity? Finally, do you design an organization-wide measurement system from the bottom-up or from the top-down?

1) Measuring Multi-Dimensional Performances

One-dimensional performance measurement.

My first performance improvement assignment was to improve the productivity of item-processing clerks at a bank. The item processors read checks and deposits and key-entered the written data to create bar codes which the bank's equipment could read. They then verified the balances of 'batches' of checks and deposits collected by the bank's branches. The historical average processing rate was 1100 items per production hour. A standard deviation above this rate was 1700 items, which became the goal. The processors were informed of their rate at the end of each day and could then compute their earnings. The incentive opportunity was a modest five percent of base pay at goal, with increments of five percent below the goal to a zero payout at 1100 items.

The results were remarkable. Within three weeks, the net rate (items minus errors) increased from the original 1100 items per hour, to an average 1650 items per hour (a 50% gain). The program remained effective for over a year. At that time the department supervisor was promoted. The new supervisor chose not to provide the processors with the daily feedback on their rates. This resulted in a decline in performance to 1150 items per hour – almost back to the original rate.

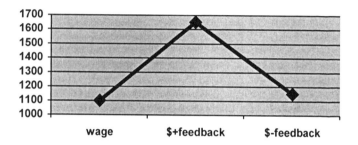

At that time, it was decided to convert the processor pay to 'piece rate'. The items per hour were divided into the average hourly wage to compute the incentive value of an item. After the introduction of the piece-rate plan, the average net item rate increased to an astonishing 3100 items an hour – a 281% gain over the original rate.

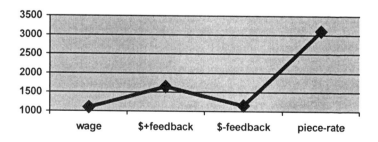

The processor piece-rate incentive plan appeared to be a remarkable success. Turnover was reduced from 150% a year to zero, due to the increased pay opportunity and employee empowerment. The supervisor, who had been a top processor, quit supervising and returned to processing, where she could earn more pay. Clearly, the employees were empowered and more satisfied, as evidenced by reductions in turnover, absenteeism, and tardiness.

The drawbacks to the plan surfaced when the operations senior manager visited the department to see first hand its effects on the employees. He sat with an operator and asked her if the plan was too stressful and would she prefer to return to a conventional hourly wage. During the discussion, the operator continued to key items and finally turned to the manager and said, "You've cost me about eight bucks – do you have a lot more to say?"

Other findings included an unwillingness on the part of the operators to train new employees, attend meetings, or assist in other areas. Basically, operators were emphatically opposed to any assignments other than key entry – understandable given the nature of the piece rate incentive plan. I was not initially discouraged by these findings and designed piece-rate plans for seven other banks.

The dramatic increases were always attained, but the side effects became more pronounced with each application. Incidents occurred where operators were arriving at work early, or skipping lunch, to enable them to obtain large quantities of items to be processed. Some operators actually hid items to ensure sufficient work volume. Other operators picked over the various item batches to find the easiest ones to process. Operators were also very opposed to hiring new operators – even when the department was unable to meet its deadlines.

In sum, piece rates are highly focused incentive plans that usually produce high levels of performance. However, they can create conflicts between employee goals and the organization's, generate competition among employees, and reduce employee willingness to assist the organization in activities other than the measured behavior.

Some years later, I was asked to assist a manufacturing plant in revamping its incentive plan for some 800 factory workers. The plan consisted of a modest base wage, plus a piece rate above a minimum item processing threshold. The plan had been in effect for three years and had dramatically increased productivity. However, the plant manager's strategy was to move to 'Just In Time' inventory to reduce inventory costs. In effect, the manager was asking me to tell 800 piece-rate employees to quit making pieces when the plant didn't need them. This proved to be an impossible assignment.

A more common example of piece rate is the sales commission plan. Essentially it pays in the same way as piece rate – especially 'straight commission' sales incentive plans. In many cases I find organizations dissatisfied with sales commission plans based entirely on revenue generation. Such plans often: encourage salespeople to sell the products that are easiest to sell rather than strategically important; to discount prices to ensure the sale while reducing gross margin to unacceptable levels; to sell things to customers who fail to pay promptly; and to make promises to customers that cannot be met by operations. Similar to piece rates, sales commissions are usually effective in generating revenue, but the adverse side effects may outweigh the benefits. Further, just as I experienced with piece rate, leveraged, commissioned salespeople often balk at assignments other than direct selling, and compete with other salespeople as well as finance and operations.

A final example illustrates the disconnect one-dimensional plans create between the employee and the organization. I was asked to design an incentive plan for two bank vault tellers. The goal was to process a certain number of items each day. The two employees had been with the bank over 30 years and were pleasant, elderly ladies. After the plan had been in effect a few weeks, the operations manager and I returned to get the two ladies' impressions of the plan. They said they liked the additional money and found the plan made the job more interesting. However, they could not understand why the bank had implemented the plan. There were not enough items for both of them to meet the daily item production goal. So, one of them processed all the items on one day and the other all the items on alternate days. In this way they received a payment every other day, where if they had both worked, they would not have earned any incentive. Not only was this solution of no value to the bank, it violated the necessary 'dual control' required in this area in which they were supposed to each process half the items – never all of the items.

To summarize, one-dimensional plans are never optimal, because all work includes at least two dimensions – production and quality. Measuring and paying on one dimension almost always has adverse consequences on the other dimension. One dimensional plans, particularly where pay is leveraged (below market pay), often cause employees to focus on maximizing personal earnings, rather than participating in the overall strategy of the organization. Finally, these plans may generate a lack of cooperation between employees, which has an overall negative effect on the department's or organization's performance.

Unconsolidated, Multi-Dimensional Measurement Plans.

Based on our experiences with one-dimensional measurements, we abandoned such plans in favor of multi-dimensional plans. In designing a plan for a target job position – quality, timeliness, costs, regulatory compliance, and other factors were considered in addition to productivity. A unique measure was developed for each important performance dimension. A specified amount of incentive pay opportunity was then assigned to each measure. A sample unconsolidated sales plan might be:

Measure	Goal	Incentive Pay at Goal
Sales Revenue	$30,000	10% of salary
# Prospects Seen	25	5% of salary
Gross Profit Margin	9%	5% of salary
% Accounts Past Due	4%	5% of salary

The above sample plan, sometimes termed 'goal sharing,' pays incentives for the percentage of goal achieved above the threshold for each of the measures <u>independently</u>. For example, in the above plan, the salesperson could fail to sell anything, but by achieving the other goals still earn a 15% (5%+5%+5%) of base pay incentive. Or, the person could achieve the sales goals through reactive selling, producing a poor margin, or creating collections problems and still receive a 10% of salary incentive payment.

Even if there is no incentive pay attached to the measures, the plan generates four unique 'scores' that must then be interpreted in some way to provide an overall performance assessment. The problem with this approach to measurement is that the measures are assessed independently, rather than consolidated to create a single score that considers all aspects of performance.

Consolidated Multi-Dimensional Performance Measurement Plans.

Time Logs. One approach to measurement is to have employees record how much time they spend on various activities. Goals are set for the percentage of time spent on key activities. The obvious problem is that there is no way to validate the data submitted by employees. Further, the time spent does not necessarily mean that organizational priorities were addressed. Another problem is that time spent can be increased without producing any results. Time logs may inadvertently reward reduced productivity, since increased time is the opposite of increased productivity.

Standard Time. Our earliest attempt at consolidating multiple dimensions was to apply industrial engineering 'standard times' to the performance measures. Each unique performance outcome is assigned a standard time value (the average time taken to complete the task). When an employee completes the outcome, they are awarded the outcome's standard time, which is then termed 'earned time.' Errors made by the employee are debited from the earned time in order to compute net or adjusted earned time. Earned time can then be compared to actual time to compute a productivity ratio.

For example, a typist might have the following standard time values assigned to his work.

Outcome	Standard Time	Completed	Earned Time
Memo	15'	4	60'
Standard Page	5'	30	150'
Technical Page	10'	30	300'
Total Earned Minutes			510'
Error Revision	10'	5	-50'
Net Earned Minutes			460'

Net Earned Hours = 460 / 60 = <u>7.67</u> hours
Actual Hours   8.00 hours

Productivity % = 95%

Standard time systems require that work be broken down to discrete activities, so they can be converted to common time values. This process is very time consuming and difficult to administer. For example, one of our client's operations had around 800 employees but over 1,000 standard time definitions. The larger problem, however, was that performance on only a small number of job dimensions can be effectively measured this way.

Conventional standard time systems do not address sales, expense control, cash flow, regulatory compliance, or customer service adequately. This became painfully obvious to us when the productivity of a group of employees ultimately exceeded 100%, but production was almost never meeting customer deadlines! Similar to piece rate, the standard time approach to performance measurement is applicable in only a small number of situations.

Performance Point. An alternative method for consolidating multiple measures is the performance points system. Points are assigned to each target employee outcome based upon some combination of the estimated time involved, the value to the organization, the aversiveness of the task, and the skills required to complete the task. The points earned on each task are aggregated to compute total points earned for a pre-defined time period.

This approach to performance measurement was outlined in B. F. Skinner's utopian novel, *Walden Two*, in which members of an experimental community received points for a wide variety of tasks from farming to playing the cello. Later, points were applied in actual mental health hospitals in what were called 'token economies.' As critics of the book charged, the valuing of various outcomes was highly subjective and sometimes arbitrary.

Nevertheless, the points system worked for some of our clients, even in reasonably complex organizations. Two unsolvable problems with the approach were that total earned points was an abstraction with which many managers could not become comfortable, and the inability of the points system to provide useful diagnostic data to guide improvement projects. A sample points system for a customer service representative is presented below. This variation involves expert raters assigning a rating from 1 = low to 10 = high, for each dimension.

	Time	Value	Difficulty	Skills	Total Points
Answer customer inquiry	3	6	5	4	18
Complete customer order	5	8	3	3	19
Resolve customer problem	8	8	7	5	28
Order error	8	8	3	3	22
Cross-sell additional products	3	10	8	9	30

The Performance Matrix. Felix and Riggs, two industrial engineers at the University of Oregon Productivity Center, first proposed a technique they termed the Performance Matrix for consolidating multiple performance measures. The performance matrix uses a 'conversion scale' to convert any type of ordinal performance to a common measurement scale. The converted scales are then weighted and summed to compute a composite 'performance index.' We renamed the performance matrix, the more familiar 'performance scorecard' and began using it in the mid 1980s in a wide variety of organizations. This approach to consolidated, multi-dimensional measurement has proven effective in even the most complex situations. Over the past 15 years we have assisted in the design of over 9,000 unique performance scorecards. The performance scorecard is discussed in detail in chapters 3 and 5.

2) Activity vs. Outcome Measurement

Activity vs. Outcome. Activities refer to the sub-outcomes that lead up to an outcome or result of value to the organization. In the process of designing performance measures, it is easy to fall into this 'activity trap.' This approach to measurement is favorably received by those to whom the measure will apply. Before we realized the ineffectiveness of this approach, we had designed a number of activity measures in various organizations. There was a high degree of employee buy-in for these activity measures, but they proved difficult to track, and failed to produce any substantive gains for the organization. Employees were often at 100% of the goals, with no real improvement in organizational performance.

In the early 80s, we immersed ourselves in activity level measurement. We defined all a job's activities and assigned standard time values to them. Each time the employee completed an activity, they earned the activity's standard time. These were summed for the day to compute 'earned time.' Due to this focus on activity, a simple result such as 'teeth cleaned' became 'supplies secured,' 'toothpaste opened,' 'tooth brush prepared,' 'water temperature adjusted,' 'teeth brushed,' 'mouth rinsed,' 'mouth dried,' 'mouth inspected,' 'supplies cleaned', and 'supplies put away.'

Employees prefer measures based on activity because they have more control over these measures. Outcome measures may be influenced by variables not under the direct control of the employee. Examples include variations in work volume, work complexity, work arrival time, materials quality, staffing levels, interruptions, off-task assignments, and internal or external customer demand changes.

Opportunity Adjusted Measures. An opportunity-adjusted measure compensates for changes in the opportunity to perform by stating the desired result as a ratio to the opportunity, or by adjusting the goal. For example, one of the measures we designed for customer service representatives (CSRs) was a 'cross-sell' measure. The number of products sold was divided by the number of customers seen. (An outcome measure would have been total products sold.) The measure's performance improved significantly, but profitability failed to increase correspondingly. An analysis of the cross-sell ratio denominator, found that a surprising number of CSRs were only serving one or two customers a day! Therefore, the total product sales were only marginally impacted by the improvement.

This case study illustrates the problem with opportunity adjusted measures. A CSR sells one product to one customer each day. When incentive pay is introduced, the CSR sells 2 products to one customer each day – a 100% improvement in performance and a maximum incentive payout, but a modest 20 additional products per month. A second CSR sells one product to ten customers per day. When incentive pay is introduced, she sells an average 1.5 products per customer – a 50% improvement, that earns half the incentive payout of the first CSR, but is a significant 100 additional products per month. The first CSR also has more time to sell, due to the number of customers served. The incentive payouts are patently unfair to the higher contributor. Measuring total products sold would have identified these performance differences and prompted a review of staffing and utilization, or encouraged the implementation of a prospecting program.

Opportunity can also be adjusted for by changing the goal. This adjustment is often made by organizations with substantial work volume cycles – especially seasonal businesses. Different goals are set for each phase of the cycle, or performance is compared to the same period, previous year. Adjusting goals for cycles, does not encourage a solution to the underlying problems of ineffective staffing or employee utilization. A more fundamental problem, however, is that cyclic goal adjustments disconnect the employee from the way the business actually operates. The chart below illustrates this problem.

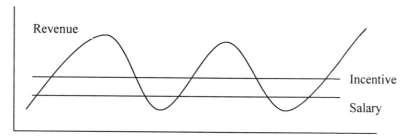

Adjusting the goal creates a constant incentive payout, even though the organization's true financials vary significantly from cycle to cycle. The employee is not aligned with ownership and management and is not motivated to solve the problem.

Behavior or Process Measures. Activity measures may also be sub-components of an outcome. For example, a trainer measurement could be that a training program is developed and delivered on time. These two measures appear to be largely under the direct control of the trainer. However, the trainer may be assigned other tasks that interfere with preparation time. To factor this variable out, we could measure training modules completed on schedule, rather than the entire training program. Training delivered on time is also dependent on whether the training is developed on time. To factor this variable out, we could measure training delivered within ten days of development. Of course, delivering training assumes trainees will attend on the scheduled training day. To factor out this variable, we would have to eliminate the deadline altogether.

Below are some examples of common activity measures and the reasons they may fail to yield real results.

Measure Category	Measure	Potential Problem
Sales	prospects seen	salesperson visits easy--to- schedule, low sales probability prospects
Expense Control	% budget	manager may negotiate the budget or postpone critical expenditures
Productivity	efficiency	employees can increase processing speed without changed work schedule or staffing level
Cash Flow	collection calls	employee calls easy to reach customers who typically do not have significant collections problems
Customer Service	% schedule	schedules are revised to reflect internal delays, customer still does not receive the order when promised

The solution is to measure outcomes whenever practical. However, the number and frequency of uncontrollable external variables should be considered in establishing the measure's goal.

Outcomes and Employee Empowerment. Activity measures do not parallel the market at large. A self-employed person is rewarded only for results. When we drift toward activity measurement, we begin to lose the critical analog to the free market. For outcome measures to be effective, employees must be given a high degree of personal discretion in how they go about producing the outcome. The self-employed person is not subject to constant, involuntary reassignments by a manager. The self-employed person does not have to follow to the letter prescribed procedures. The self-employed person does not require permission to address issues in novel ways. Not only are outcome measures more effective for the organization, ultimately they empower the employee. This is so because activity measures are more intrusive, in that they dictate how things are to be accomplished. Further, outcome measures, more so than activity, tie the employee more closely to the business strategy of the organization, since they more directly affect it.

Analyzing and Improving Outcomes With Activity Component Measures. A useful application of activity measures is to pinpoint the causes of low performance outcomes and to provide more contemporaneous and targeted performance feedback to employees. For example, sales revenue is an outcome measure. If sales are not meeting the goal, we must determine the cause of this deficiency. Measuring prospecting, closing, cross-sell, and vertical-sell will help us identify the root cause of low sales, and guide the development of a tactical improvement plan. Normally, we would not pay incentives for improvements in these activities. However, improvements in the activities are reinforced by improvements in sales, which then earns incentive pay.

3. Bottom-Up vs. Top-Down Measurement Strategies

Bottom-Up: Piece-meal Measurement and Incentive Pay Implementations. In his book, *Human Competence*, Tom Gilbert proposed that decisions to measure performance should be determined by the measure's 'Performance Improvement Potential' or PIP. Temporary measures would identify high-improvement opportunity behaviors, and measures would be implemented to capitalize on the opportunity. This approach is a formalized statement of the way many organizations decide where to implement performance measurement and incentive pay plans. Measures, and sometimes incentives, are introduced to solve a specific problem. They are introduced 'piecemeal,' rather than from a total system perspective.

The dangers associated with this piecemeal approach are several. Since only the problem issue is measured, other dimensions of the job may become worse, as employees and managers focus exclusively on the one dimension. Second, problems which may be critical at the line level, may in fact, have a rather negligible impact on the organization's strategy. Third, this incremental approach to the implementation of measurement and incentive pay, creates a hodge-podge measurement system which provides little overall organizational direction. Finally, the piecemeal approach, in a real sense, rewards poor performance by triggering the implementation of incentive pay, while it ignores high-performing areas.

Bottom-Up: System Process Measurement and Incentive Pay Implementations. Some management theorists argue that a systems process approach to defining performance measures should be adopted. The model, in its simplest form, is:

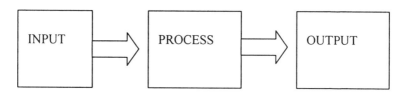

The system process is mapped from input through output. Productivity, quality, and timeliness measures are applied at each critical juncture of the workflow, from input through process to output. This approach is useful for improving a process, but still focuses on the activity without consideration of the overarching financial and strategic objectives of the organization. The chief problem with measuring activity or process is that activity, in and of itself, may have little or no value to the organization. 'Busyness isn't Business'. In fact, a focus on current activity will often constrain the development of creative alternatives to improving the financial and strategic performance of the organization. Today's business environment changes rapidly and the traditional 'job description' or 'process map' is always playing 'catch-up' with what the organization is actually doing. Process charting and improvement is, however, a valuable 'Tactical Improvement Plan'.

Employee Involvement Strategies. Many management theorists argue that the line employee should be directly involved in the development of performance measures to ensure a sense of empowerment and to gain employee acceptance of the plan. "Those closest to the work know best how to measure it", is the position taken. Line employees, however, are typically not provided consistent information on the strategic direction of the organization. Furthermore, employees will often insist on measuring processes and behaviors rather than outcomes, because they have more control over them.

The unfortunate result of employee sponsored design is a measurement system that is perceived as very fair, but fails to improve the performance of the organization. In designing a performance measurement system, it is helpful to view the manager as the customer and the subordinate as the vendor. It is the customer who decides what is important and what he wants to pay for – not the vendor!

Strategy-Based Measurement System Implementations. Many performance measurement and incentive pay plans use the current job description as a starting point. The designer of a sales incentive plan wants more revenue. But the questions should be asked: "More revenue from which product lines?, from which customers?, in which territories?, at what margin?, with what credit risk?, at the expense of what customer service issues?, and at what production and marketing costs?". These are *strategic* issues for the organization. They must be approached from a strategic point of view rather than a process or activity view.

In their book "*The Balanced Scorecard,*" Kaplan and Norton describe an approach to designing performance measurement systems they term the 'method of cascading objectives.' An organizational 'strategic' scorecard is designed based upon the strategic plan, vision statement, or other planning tools. The strategic scorecard designers must consider customers, vendors, competitors, ownership and stockholders, management, and workers in selecting the best collection of strategic measures. The strategic scorecard then serves as a guide, or blueprint, for the design of all other performance measures.

Designing scorecards beginning with senior management, then middle management, line management, and finally staff and workers ensures that the performance dimensions and priorities established in the strategic scorecard are continued through all other scorecards at each organizational level. This 'method of cascading objectives' ensures measures are aligned throughout the organization.

The cascading objectives measurement strategy is much more efficient than the bottom-up approach, and creates a system which is much easier to evaluate and administer. We designed an organization-wide performance system for a medium-sized organization using the bottom-up, piecemeal approach. There were some 110 unique job positions, so there could be as many as 110 unique measurement plans. After four years of fairly continuous design effort, we had managed to design measurement and incentive pay plans for around 70 of the job positions. Each plan met the goals of its unique design manager and employees. Plans were tracked on spreadsheets in each department.

At the end of the fourth year, it was decided that a comprehensive review of all the plans should be performed. Since data were tracked in each department, and recorded in a fashion unique to the department, it took several months to gather all the data. In reviewing the results, the only common data were the actual incentive payouts. To evaluate performance improvements proved quite difficult due to the variety of methods used in designing and tracking the plans. After several weeks of meeting, the comprehensive review was abandoned, even though substantial incentive payouts were made to the 500 employees.

Some years later, we were asked to assist in the design of a performance measurement and incentive pay system for an organization that was very similar in size, ownership, products, and number of employees and branches to the one described above. However, the cascading objectives method was employed to design the new organization's measures. Using this method, measures were designed for some 90 unique job positions over a three-week period (in contrast to four years using the piecemeal method). The system's effectiveness could be evaluated monthly by simply reviewing performance improvements on the strategic scorecard. If a strategic measure was not improving, it was a simple task to drill down through the measurement levels to pinpoint the obstacles for improvement.

In conclusion, we are recommending the introduction of results-oriented, multiple measures presented in the performance scorecard format. Furthermore, it is recommended that the top-down, cascading objectives method be employed in the design of the measurement system. The remainder of the book is based on these recommendations.

Chapter 5

Case Study: Design of a Restaurant Total Performance System

Bill's Place: A Case Study

Description.

Bill founded his restaurant ten years ago. Bill had invested $600,000 in his original restaurant, plus a proposed new location, and wants to receive a minimum return of 15% a year on his investment. The restaurant operates seven days a week, opens at 11:00 A.M., and closes at 11:00 P.M. The featured menu items are prime rib, steaks, and select wines.

Strategy.

Bill's strategies are:

1) To control expenses in order to increase gross profits.
2) To provide consistently high-quality food in an attractive and spotless atmosphere.
3) To prospect for company events, birthdays, reunions, and other group functions.
4) To open a second restaurant in the west end of town by the end of the year.

Payroll.

Job Position	average hourly pay	average annual pay	average monthly pay
2 mgrs	---	$40,000	$3,333
1 event orgr	---	$18,000	$1,500
2 hostesses	$8.50/hr	---	$1,122
12 food servers	$6.00/hr	---	$ 972
3 bussers	$5.50/hr	---	$ 880
3 cocktail serv	$5.00/hr	---	$ 840
2 bartenders	$9.00/hr	---	$1,188
1 bookkeeper		$24,000	$2,000
26 employees			

Job Descriptions.

Lunch Shift Manager.
- Prepare weekly staffing schedules.
- Open restaurant for business.
- Ensure all staff are present and assigned to areas.
- Conduct pre-opening quality walk-through.
- Initialize point-of-sales machines and ensure adequate change.
- Order and check in supplies and food stuffs.
- Sign out staff.
- Audit service and product.
- Greet customers.
- Approve checks.
- Close down shift, run end-of-shift financials.
- Inform dinner manager of issues.
- Assist in opening second restaurant.

Dinner Shift Manager.
- Prepare weekly staffing schedules.
- Ensure all staff are present and assigned to areas.
- Conduct pre and post shift quality walk-through.
- Initialize point-of-sales machines and ensure adequate change.
- Sign out staff.
- Audit service and product.
- Greet customers.
- Approve checks.
- Close down shift, run end-of-shift and end-of-day financials.
- Inform lunch manager of issues.
- Assist in opening second restaurant.

Event Organizer.
- Prepare event menus, pricing, and contracts.
- Order special request food and beverage items.
- Inform shift managers of coming events with two weeks lead-time.
- Visit groups to promote group events at restaurant.
- Telemarket and manage advertising for group events.
- Supervise group events with more than 15 customers.
- Train staff in servicing group events.
- Procure group event specialty items.

Hostess.
- Prepare hostess stand at beginning of shift.
- Make phone reservations.
- Greet customers.
- Maintain waiting list.
- Seat customers to ensure balanced sections.
- Maintain seating chart and customer counts.

- Walk through restaurant to identify unmet customer needs.
- Assist food servers as available.
- Inform shift manager of issues.
- Thank customers as they leave and inquire about service.

Foodserver.

- Greet customers and provide menus.
- Describe food specials.
- Answer customer questions about the menus.
- Take beverage orders.
- Submit orders to kitchen.
- Enter tab to point-of-sale register.
- Take beverage orders to customers.
- Take meal orders.
- Submit meal order to kitchen with any special instructions highlighted.
- Compare meals to orders and instructions and correct.
- Take orders to customers.
- Visit table to get customer requests.
- Describe desserts and take orders.
- Deliver orders.
- Prepare bill at customer's request.
- Enter payment (get check approval from shift manager).
- Return receipt and credit card or change.
- Thank customer.

Busser.

- Conduct pre-shift housekeeping audit.
- Prepare bus stand.
- Prepare section tables.
- When customers are seated, bring bread and water.
- Replenish bread and water as required.

- Bus unneeded dishes and utensils.
- Assist server in bringing large orders.
- When customer leaves, clean and reset table.
- Thank customer.
- Maintain section housekeeping.
- Inspect and remove all unclean utensils.
- Assist kitchen when possible.

Cocktail Server.
- Hand out wine list after customer is seated.
- Describe cocktail and wine specials.
- Answer questions about cocktails and wine.
- Take cocktail orders.
- Submit cocktail orders to bartender.
- Enter purchases to P.O.S. tab.
- Garnish orders.
- Deliver orders to customers.
- When food order is completed, take recommendations and take wine orders.
- Get wine from storage, present to customer for inspection, open wine.
- Enter purchase to P.O.S. tab.
- When meal is finished, inquire about after-dinner, beverages.

Bartender.
- Perform walk-through inspection at start of shift.
- Stock bar and bring out bottles.
- Prepare garnishes & mixes.
- Ensure P.O.S. is initialized with adequate change.
- Take bar orders, prepare and serve drinks.
- Take cocktail server orders, prepare and serve drinks.
- Enter orders to P.O.S.

- Process cash and charge cards.
- Maintain bar appearance and cleanliness.

Cook.
- Conduct pre-shift kitchen and storage quality walk-throughs.
- Review inventory and inform manager of shortages or spoilage.
- Prepare ovens.
- Prepare condiments and produce.
- Take orders from food servers and prepare meals.
- Clean utensils and dinnerware.

Bookkeeper.
- Reconcile P.O.S. with cash and credit cards.
- Update general ledger.
- Prepare daily deposits for manager.
- Check inventory weekly and order stock.
- Pay bills.
- Prepare bills for special events.
- Make collections calls.
- Prepare financial reports.
- Record and audit time sheet hours.
- Record tips for IRS.
- Compute weekly payroll, prepare payroll report and checks.
- Assist in opening second restaurant.

Financials
For Period Ending in June

Revenue	Current YTD	Previous YTD	% Chg
Lunch Food	118,440	131,400	(10%)
Dinner Food	731,817	754,584	(3%)
Lunch Bev	37,835	40,500	(7%)
Dinner Bev	105,973	112,777	(6%)
Lunch Wine	16,450	20,700	(25%)
Dinner Wine	99,975	180,444	(80%)
Lunch L/B	29,610	28,800	2%
Dinner L/B	139,965	114,828	17%
Lunch Rev	202,335	221,400	(9%)
Dinner Rev	1,077,730	1,162,633	(7%)
Total Rev	1,280,065	1,384,033	(8%)

Cost of Sales	Current YTD	% Rev	Previous YTD	% Rev
Food	510,154	60%	442,992	50%
Beverage	43,142	30%	47,516	31%
Wine	23,285	20%	52,297	26%
Liquor/Beer	50,873	30%	41,652	29%
Cost of Sales	627,454	49%	584,457	42%
Gross Profit	652,611	51%	799,576	58%

	Current YTD	% Rev	Previous YTD	% Rev
General Expenses				
Wages/Salaries	179,868	14%	181,325	13%
Benefits	43,168	3%	43,518	3%

Kitchen Suply	6,800	0.50%	5,950		0.40%
Other Suply	3,210	0.20%	4,200		0.30%
Utilities	1,125	0.08%	985		0.07%
Build Maint	675	0.05%	679		0.05%
Training Exp	0	0.00%	0		0.00%
Gen Exp	234,846	18.0%	236,657		17.0 %
Interest Exp	35,000	2.7%	39,400		2.8 %

Net Pre-Tax

Income   382,765   29.9%   523,519   37.8%

DESIGN STEPS

1) Design strategic scorecard.
2) Assign measure categories on the organization-wide scorecard blueprint.
3) Assign measure categories and weights for all levels of the blueprint.
4) Design measures for each assigned category, and 'cascade' measures and weights down through each successive organizational level.
5) Identify or develop data sources for each performance measure.
6) Determine profit funding pool(s) for incentive pay plan.
7) Define funding controllable net income or productivity ratio.
8) Define the 'multiplier' scale threshold.
9) Define the multiplier scale range and intervals.
10) Test the historical incentive opportunity and revise as needed.
11) Define the performance measures bases and goals using:
    a) strategic objective goals
    b) target multiplier level
    c) budgets
    d) statistical methods
    e) 30% rule

12) Prepare System Documentation, set up reporting database, and conduct test run.

IMPLEMENTATION STEPS

1) Conduct *Management Practices* survey.
2) Review analysis and survey results to pinpoint obstacles to a successful implementation.
3) Develop an implementation plan that overcomes the obstacles to include changes in:
   a) job roles
   b) communications
   c) supervision
   d) conventional pay practices
   e) selection methods and/or criteria
   f) training
   g) performance evaluations
   h) promotions
4) Train managers and supervisors in the system mechanics and 'positive leadership.'
5) Conduct team meetings to explain the system to employees and to develop Tactical Improvement Plans.
6) Perform three- and six-month reviews.

Design Steps

STEP 1: Develop the Strategic Scorecard.

Review the strategic objectives. The objectives should be neither redundant nor incompatible. One or more measurable outcomes is defined for each strategic objective. Measures are quantifiable and data should allow for monthly reporting.

Objective	Base	Goal	Weight
1) Gross profit margin %	51%	58%	30%
2) Average customer service survey rating (7-point scale)	3.6	6.0	20%
3) Event and group function sales	$7,000	$10,000	30%
4) Project Milestone Timeliness	80%	100%	20%

STEP 2: Assign measure categories on the Organization-wide scorecard blueprint.

Write the organizational objectives from step 1, above the related measure category(s). Then enter the priority weight for each cell for which a measure will be defined.

ORG OBJ		REV	PROD	EXP	CASH FLOW	CUST. SERV	REGUL COMP	STRAT PROJ
ORG OBJ			Gross profit 15%	Gross profit 15%				
ORG OBJ						Cust. Serv 20%		
ORG OBJ		Event sales 30%						New unit 20%
JOB TITLE		REV	PROD	EXP	CASH FLOW	CUST. SERV	REGUL COMP	STRAT PROJ
LUNCH MGR			20%	20%		30%		30%
DIN MGR			20%	20%		30%		30%
EVENT ORG		70%				30%		
HOST			50%			50%		
FOOD SERVER		30%	20%	10%		40%		
CKTAIL SERVER		30%	20%	10%		40%		
BAR TEND		30%	20%	10%		40%		
BUSSER			50%			50%		
COOK			20%	30%		50%		
BOOK KEEPR				50%				50%

STEPS 3 and 4: Define performance measures and weights for the senior management level of the blueprint and then cascade measures down through each successive organizational level.

Position Name: *Lunch Manager*

#	MEASURE NAME	WT	BASE	GOAL
1	Lunch Shift Labor Cost / Revenue	20%	$12.30	$13.50
2	Lunch Food Cost / Revenue	20%	$7.38	$6.75
3	Lunch Shift Average Customer Survey Rating	30%	3.8	6.0
4	New Restaurant Project Milestones	30%	80%	100%

Position Name: *Dinner Manager*

#	MEASURE NAME	WT	BASE	GOAL
1	Dinner Shift Labor Cost / Revenue	20%	$28.34	$31.15
2	Dinner Food Cost / Revenue	20%	$17.00	$15.60
3	Dinner Shift Average Customer Survey Rating	30%	3.5	6.0
4	New Restaurant Project Milestones	30%	80%	100%

Position Name: *Event Organizer*

	MEASURE NAME	WT	BASE	GOAL
1	Event Revenue	70%	$7,000	$10,000
2	Event Customer Service Average Rating	30%	4.0	6.0

Position Name: *Hostess*

	MEASURE NAME	WT	BASE	GOAL
1	Shift Meals / Labor Hour	50%	4.0	4.5
2	Customer Survey Average Rating	50%	3.6	6.0

Position Name: *Food Server*

	MEASURE NAME	WT	BASE	GOAL
1	Add-on Sales per Meal	30%	$2.50	$3.20
2	Meals per Labor Hour	20%	4.0	4.5
3	Returns per Meal	10%	5%	1%
4	Customer Service Average Server Rating	40%	3.6	6.0

Position Name: *Cocktail Server*

	MEASURE NAME	WT	BASE	GOAL
1	Wine/Liquor Sales per Meal	30%	1.84	2.25
2	Wine/Liquor Sales per Labor Hour	20%	$18.10	$21.00
3	Returns per Meal	10%	12%	1%
4	Customer Service Average Server Rating	40%	2.8	6.0

Position Name: *Bartender*

	MEASURE NAME	WT	BASE	GOAL
1	Sales per Bar Customer	30%	5.50	6.50
2	Liquor/Wine Sales per Labor Hour	20%	$19.10	$21.00
3	Liquor/Wine Gross Profit	20%	35%	40%
4	Customer Service Average Server Rating	40%	2.8	6.0

Position Name: *Busser*

	MEASURE NAME	WT	BASE	GOAL
1	Meals per Labor Hour	50%	4.0	4.5
2	Customer Service Average Team Rating	50%	3.6	6.0

Position Name: *Cook*

	MEASURE NAME	WT	BASE	GOAL
1	Meals per Labor Hour	20%	5.0	5.5
2	Food Gross Profit per Meal	30%	32%	40%
3	Returns per Meal (customer service measures)	30%	8%	2%
4	Customer Service Average Food Rating	20%	5.2	6.0

Position Name: *Bookkeeper*

	MEASURE NAME	WT	BASE	GOAL
1	Percent Reports on Time	30%	80%	100%
2	% Discounts Taken	20%	40%	80%
3	New Restaurant Project Milestones	50%	80%	100%

STEP 5: Identify or develop data sources for each performance measure.

The data element sources (where data is found), and who will be responsible for reporting the data each month, were defined. Existing data sources were used when possible. In some cases, a measure is used in more than one scorecard. In these instances, a single data source and person would report the measure's data.

Step 6: Determine funding pool(s) for incentive pay plan.

The funding pool is the source of funds for the incentive plan. Funding pools can be computed at the Holding Company, organizational, business line, and divisional or profit center level. Bill's restaurant will be funded at the organizational level given it is a small organization. When the additional restaurant is operational, a decision will have to be made about whether to fund from the aggregate results or the results of each restaurant.

Step 7: Define controllable net income.

The restaurant management team reviewed the financial statement and decided that there were no significant uncontrollable revenues or expense. They therefore chose the actual net income of the restaurant as the funding source for incentive pay. This decision will be reviewed when the new restaurant is added to the income statement.

Step 8: Define the incentive pay scale threshold.

The incentive pay scale net income threshold is the zero incentive pay-out level. It is defined as the sum of the average monthly uncontrollable expenses, minimum return on investment to ownership, debt pay down, and reserve. Since the restaurant's actual net income will be used to compute incentive pay opportunity, there are no 'uncontrollable expenses' to consider in setting the threshold.

Bill has invested $600,000 in his original restaurant and wants to receive a minimum return of 15% a year on his investment ($7,500 a month). In addition, Bill wants to set aside a monthly $2,500 reserve to cover expenses associated with opening the new restaurant. The monthly incentive pay multiplier scale threshold will be:

Threshold = $7,500 + $2,500 = $10,000

Step 9: Define the multiplier scale range and intervals.

Step A: Define employee basis percentage.

A 'basis percentage' is assigned to each employee for a period of one year. The basis percentage is the percentage of base pay that, when multiplied by the incentive pay multiplier, defines the employee's incentive pay opportunity for the month. For example, an employee with a basis percentage of 5%, would have a 15% of base pay incentive opportunity when the multiplier was at 3.0 (5% x 3.0 = 15%). The same basis percentage may be assigned to all employees, or the decision may be to assign higher bases to management, critical job positions, or underpaid job positions. Bill decided to provide a 10% basis for his shift managers and a 5% basis for all other employees.

Step B: Define multiplier scale range.

The multiplier scale can range from zero to infinity. If the lowest scale point on the range is zero, then at that level of CNI, there will be no incentive pay opportunity, regardless of scorecard performance. A lowest scale range of one, means that a 'budgeted' opportunity is provided that is unrelated to organizational profitability. The upper range is often set at three times the lower range.

Bill and the management team decided to set the incentive pay multiplier scale range from 0 to 3.00.

Step C: Compute the incentive pay liability for a multiplier interval of 1.00.

Given the basis percentage(s) and scale range they selected, the following table lists the incentive pay opportunities for the restaurant employees when the multiplier is at 1.00.

Job Position	Number Emps.	Monthly Base Pay	Incentive Basis %	Incentive Opp at 1.00
Shift Manager	2	$3,333	10%	$ 667
Event Organizer	1	1,500	5%	75
Hostess	2	1,122	5%	112
Food Server	12	972	5%	583
Busser	3	880	5%	132
Cocktail Server	3	840	5%	126
Bartender	2	1,188	5%	119
Cook	3	1,400	5%	210
Bookkeeper	1	2,000	5%	100

Total Incentive Liability at 1.0 Multiplier = $2,124 = $2,000 rounded

Step D: Define the CNI (net income) value for the 1.00 multiplier interval.

1) Define the 'share percentage.' The share percentage is the percentage of each dollar over the threshold that will be allocated to incentive pay funding. The share percentage can simply be decided upon by ownership or management. However, a reliable approach has been to divide total employee base pay (excluding benefits) by revenue to find the payroll's current percentage of revenue The current YTD wages and salaries is $179,868, while the current YTD revenue is $1,280,065. Payroll as a percentage of revenue is, then

Payroll as a % of revenue = $181,325 / $1,384,033 = 13%

To ensure the incentive share is equivalent to the current payroll's share percentage, we need to adjust for the fact that the scorecard indexes will lower the actual pay out. The average scorecard score across many companies has been 60%. Dividing the payroll % of revenue by .60 adjusts for the scorecard lowering of incentive earnings.

Payroll % Revenue   Adjusted Share %
13%   / .60 =   22%

2) Define the CNI required for a multiplier interval of 1.00.

From the above step, Bill divided the average total employees' monthly base pay by the adjusted share percentage to compute the CNI required for a multiplier of 1.00. The answer was: $2,000 / .22 = $9,090 = $9,000 rounded

Bill's Place Incentive Pay Multiplier Scale.

Multiplier	CNI
0.00	$10,000
0.50	14,500
1.00	19,000
1.25	21,250
1.50	23,500
1.75	25,750
2.00	28,000
2.25	30,250
2.50	32,500
2.75	34,750
3.00	37,000

STEP E: Test the historical incentive opportunity and revise as needed.

Bill then computed the current year's average monthly CNI. At least a modest incentive pay opportunity should have been available to employees. If not, he should rethink the threshold and share percentage. If these cannot be adjusted, consider a budgeted opportunity (multiplier does not fall below 1.00), for the first six months of the program.

The previous YTD average monthly pre-tax, net income was $523,519 /12 = $43,627. The average multiplier value would have exceeded 3.00. The average incentive opportunity for the employees of Bill's Place would have been 3.00 x 10% = 30% of salary for the shift managers and 3.00 x 5% = 15% of wages or salaries for all other employees. The plan would therefore, provide a very good initial incentive opportunity for employees.

STEP F: Define the performance measures bases and goals.

There are four methods for setting performance measure bases and goals:

1) Set goals that will achieve a target multiplier level – for example a 3.00.
2) Set goals to ensure conventional budgets are achieved or exceeded by some percentage.
3) Set goals statistically with the base equal to (or somewhat below) the mean, and the goal equal to one standard deviation above the mean.
4) In the absence of any other information, set goals with the base at current performance, and the goal at a thirty-percent improvement. Adjust these goals statistically when historical data become available.

Two Goal Setting Concepts.

Performance goals may be set to achieve organizational financial and strategic goals (methods 1 & 2). To 'shape' employee performance, the base must be set at, or below, current performance levels. This logic is employed when the primary purpose of the system is to improve organizational performance. Using this method, scorecard performance indexes will typically range from 30 to 60.

Alternatively, goals may be set based on historical performance to ensure employees can achieve the goals consistently (methods 3 and 4). This approach to goal setting is used when the objectives are to attract and retain good performers, and to transition toward variable pay. Using this method, scorecard performance indexes will typically range from 40 to 70.

When you statistically set the base and goal, you should consider the shape of the distribution and any performance trend. Skewed or bimodal distributions indicate the existence of performance constraints that may need to be addressed before an accurate statistical base and goal can be established. Significant performance trends across periods should also be considered, by using the standard error of the mean of the most recent data point, rather than the mean and standard deviation of the total distribution.

PRE-IMPLEMENTATION STEPS

1) Conduct a *Management Practices* survey.
2) Review analysis and survey results to pinpoint obstacles to a successful implementation.
3) Develop an implementation plan that overcomes the obstacles to include changes in:
   a) job roles
   b) communications

    c) supervision
    d) conventional pay practices
    e) selection methods and/or criteria
    f) training
    g) performance evaluations
    h) promotions
4) Implement system
5) Conduct three- and six-month system reviews

STEP 1: Conduct Management Practices Survey.

Please rate your manager on the following management practices using the scale: 1 = completely disagree, 2 = disagree, 3 = somewhat disagree, 4 = somewhat agree, 5 = agree, 6 = completely agree

Our Manager:
1. Meets at least weekly with us.
2. Keeps us informed about developments in our department.
3. Explains the organization's long-term strategy and how well it is being achieved.
4. Provides regular feedback on how we are performing compared to our goals.
5. Gives us the opportunity to try out new ideas.
6. Works with us individually to help us succeed.
7. Consistently recognizes our successes.
8. Helps us continuously improve our work methods and procedures.
9. Makes sure we have the right number of employees to get the job done.
10. Makes sure we have the needed equipment, supplies, and training to meet our goals.
11. Works effectively with upper management and other departments.
12. Works effectively with customers and suppliers.

The above survey was given to six of the restaurant employees. The results were as follow:

Item	1	2	3	4	5	6	AVG
1	1	3	2	2	1	1	1.66
2	2	1	5	2	3	3	2.66
3	1	1	2	1	2	2	1.50
4	1	1	1	2	1	1	1.16
5	3	2	3	6	6	5	4.16
6	3	3	3	4	4	3	3.33
7	6	4	3	6	4	4	4.50
8	2	6	5	5	4	4	4.33
9	1	1	2	2	3	2	1.83
10	4	5	5	4	5	3	4.33
11	6	6	5	5	6	5	5.50
12	4	5	5	4	5	3	4.16

STEP 2: Review survey results to pinpoint obstacles to a successful implementation.

Items 1, 2, 3, 4, and 9 are the management practices least applied by the management at Bill's Place. Items 1-4 are concerned with effective communications and feedback, while item 9 relates to staffing practices.

STEP 3: Develop an implementation plan that overcomes the obstacles.

Based on the survey results, communications between management and staff needs improvement. This is a critical issue for a proper implementation. Employees must understand the system and its rationale for the system to effectively improve performances. Close attention should be given to the development of orientation materials. Managers should be thoroughly trained in how to explain the system. Weekly shift meetings should be mandatory, and managers should learn how to conduct these meetings to ensure employees understand new developments, the long-term strategy, and are provided timely feedback regarding performance.

The poor responses to item 9 indicates a review of staffing procedures should precede the implementation. In particular, overstaffing would reduce scorecard performances for most of the employees.

STEP 4: Implement the System.

STEP 5: Perform three- and six-month reviews.

Chapter Six

The Method of Cascading Objectives

Performance improvement as a business strategy.

Businesses try many strategies for improving and sustaining profitability. One often overlooked strategy is employee performance improvement. Improving employee performances can have a significant and sustained impact on profitability, usually without any capital expenditure. Employee performances drive critical business objectives including sales, productivity, expense control, cash flow, customer satisfaction, regulatory compliance, and value-added projects.

A Common Sense Approach. Many organizations don't develop an employee performance improvement strategy simply because they don't know how. There are many human performance theories, and many of these theories offer conflicting views. However, underneath all this debate there are a few immutable principles which will successfully guide a performance improvement initiative. These principles are not new. They are:

1. You should have a strategy before you develop tactics.
2. What gets measured is what gets done.
3. You can't improve without doing something different.
4. People tend to do what's in their best interests.

1. You should have a strategy before you develop tactics. Before implementing a performance improvement program, an organization should convert its business strategy to an 'organizational scorecard' that consists of no more than nine organization-wide objectives. These objectives should be given priority weights, stated as quantifiable measures, and have performance compared to a base and goal (where we've been and where we want to be). The measures should be balanced to reflect financial and non-financial goals, as well as short-term and long-term objectives. The 'organizational scorecard' provides a precisely stated strategy, and a means for objectively assessing the success of the strategy.

The strategy should then be 'cascaded' down through the organization by identifying and measuring results that drive the strategy for divisions, departments, teams, or individuals. If this is done properly, the outcome will be a group of performance scorecards that describe the results needed from each employee to accomplish the overall organizational strategy.

Performance data should be collected, and feedback provided monthly, for each performance measure. This is not only good performance management, it also provides trend data. The scorecard data enable managers to pinpoint low or declining performances, and focus their limited resources on high opportunity performances.

2. What gets measured is what gets done. Sharing the scorecard results with employees provides them direction and critical performance feedback. Useful feedback must be frequent and focused. Scorecard results should be shared at least monthly to allow employees to react quickly to negative performance trends, and to make timely evaluations of the effectiveness of performance improvement tactics. Useful feedback is also focused. Performance measures that are too removed from the employee's practical ability to control are of little value in directing performance or evaluating improvement tactics. Performance feedback must also be provided for those results employees can do something about.

3. You can't improve without doing something different. Many organizations install performance feedback and/or performance pay systems with the anticipation that these systems will improve employee performances, and ultimately the success of the organization. The results are often disappointing. Management may decide that such systems don't work without examining the quality of the system they have installed. To improve employee performance, the system measures must pinpoint the drivers of strategically important results for each job position and then provide timely and focused feedback to the employee. Simply posting overall financial results, or sharing excess profits each year, does not meet these basic requirements.

However, even if an organization does provide timely, focused feedback to its employees, there will be little improvement if employees don't *do something different*. Performance improvement requires a change in processes or behaviors. An organization must assist employees in the implementation of these changes to realize significant improvements.

4. People tend to do what's in their best interests. To motivate and sustain employee performance improvements, employees should personally benefit from the improvements. Before implementing *any* improvement initiative, the developers should ask the question, "What is the personal effect of the proposed initiative on the participants?" For example, if we ask employees to improve productivity, will the result be a reduction in hours or layoffs? Improvements (doing something different) usually involve effort as well as the risk of mistakes. Possible adverse consequences to the improvement initiative should be minimized. Positive consequences should be built into the initiative, including recognition and performance pay.

All of this can be put quite simply:

Tell me what needs to be done.
Tell me how I am doing.
Help me to do better.
Share the benefits of improvement with me.

The first phase in the design of a Total Performance System, is the development of the organization-wide performance measurement system. The measurement system is the foundation of the performance system. Performance pay, and performance management, will fail if they are based on a poorly constructed measurement system. A well-designed system however will align employee performances with the organization's strategy, facilitate performance improvement, sustain optimal performance levels, and assist in fairly recognizing top performers. It should also provide management and staff a means for quickly identifying the causes of performance failures, as well as opportunities to improve the organization's performance.

Designing a Strategic Scorecard. The Method of Cascading Objectives begins with the design of an organizational or strategic scorecard. The organization's strategic plan or 'vision statement' can serve as a guide to the design of the scorecard. The measures on the strategic scorecard should be objective and quantifiable, rather than abstractions. Each measure should yield a number that can be compared to a goal. Where possible, the measures should describe a strategy – not a result. For example, net income is usually not considered a strategic measure, since it does not point to specific tactics for its achievement. The same is true of financial ratios such as return on capital, return on assets, or shareholder return. These ratios are useful diagnostic tools for investors, but provide little information about the organization's strategy for generating the return.

The measures on the strategic scorecard should 'balance' short-term and long-term goals. "Gainshare" incentive plans share expense savings with employees. This narrow focus on expense reduction can create significant adverse results for an organization in sales, service, technology enhancement, and staffing. Though more balanced than gain sharing, profit sharing plans still ignore many long-term organizational objectives. Strategic projects, customer service, employee development, and regulatory compliance may all suffer when short-term profits are the only objective.

The Seven Performance Measurement Categories. Many organizations find it difficult to translate their 'vision statements' into concrete measures. In some cases, the organization may have developed no formal strategy at all. Over the past twenty years, we have worked with hundreds of companies and assisted them in the design of over twenty-five thousand objective performance measures. As a result of these experiences, we find that performance measures can be classified into seven discrete categories. These categories can serve as a guide in the development of a strategic scorecard.

The seven performance measurement categories are:

1) Sales
2) Expense Control
3) Productivity
4) Cash Flow
5) Customer Satisfaction
6) Regulatory Compliance
7) Strategic Projects

Short-term Performance Measurement Categories.

1) Sales. The sales category includes any measures designed to directly increase revenues. Example measures are total revenue, gross profit, sales per customer, target products, territory revenue, and others.

2) Expense Control. The expense category includes all expenses, except labor expense, which is addressed in the productivity category. Targeted expenses should be those employees influence. One approach is to define all the expenses that employees can impact as an aggregate 'total controllable expenses.' Examples of controllable expenses are travel and entertainment, supplies, shrinkage, scrap, maintenance, returns, and others.

3) Productivity. Productivity is the output of employees (revenue, volume) compared to the input (labor cost, labor hours), and is almost always defined as a ratio. Examples include labor expense / revenue; revenue / employee; volume / labor hour, and others. Productivity is also affected by systemic issues, such as the timeliness and accuracy of upstream or support department performance relative to downstream departments. These relationships are often referred to as 'internal' customers and can be directly assessed through surveys, or other more objective measures. Internal customer performances are not typically applied to the strategic scorecard, but are often applied in lower level scorecards.

4) Cash Flow. Cash flow generally refers to collections, inventory and payables. These may be collectively expressed as 'Days Outstanding' using the formula Days Sales Outstanding + Days Inventory Outstanding - Days Payables Outstanding.

Long-term Performance Measurement Categories.

5) Customer Satisfaction. Customer satisfaction can be determined by customer survey ratings, or more direct measures of service timeliness and accuracy. Ratings can be obtained in a number of ways including mail surveys, customer comment cards, customer call backs, automated touch-tone telephone surveys, e-mail, Internet, and short surveys conducted by customer contact employees in sales, customer service, repair, and delivery. Customer loyalty, or account retention, is presumably predicted by customer satisfaction. Satisfaction measures are a more immediate and actionable measure of these longer-term outcomes. In this context, customers refer to external, paying customers rather than 'internal' customers.

6) Regulatory Compliance. These measures usually refer to measures of compliance with governing professional, industry or governmental agencies. Example governmental agencies are DOT, OSHA, EPA, and the IRS. Compliance measures may include checklists, audit scores, citations, fines, and others.

7) Strategic Projects. A project measure is a non-recurring measure. Once the project is completed, there is no further measurement. Projects are most often measured in terms of milestone accomplishment. Strategic projects are defined as projects which directly drive strategic measures, require a significant number of staff days, and projects that will not yield a significant benefit in the same year. Projects that do not meet these criteria, are classified as productivity related. A project timeliness measure we often employ is to evaluate milestone timeliness using the formula: (actual completion date – assigned date) / (goal completion date – assigned date).

Roll-Up Strategic Measures. In some cases, a strategic measurement category is reported at the divisional or departmental level, rather than the organizational level. For example, there may be several strategic projects. In this situation, the average performance on the sub-measures is computed and considered as the organizational performance.

Using the Seven Measurement Categories To Develop an Organizational Strategic Scorecard

STEP 1. A strategic planning group is designated. Typically, this group may include the CEO, CFO, Division Heads, HR Director, Quality Assurance, and the Strategic Planning Director.

STEP 2. The group brainstorms which categories to include on the strategic scorecard and their relative priority weightings (total equals 100%). One successful brainstorming technique for this purpose, is to have each participant independently create a list of priority weighted categories. These categories are collected and summarized on a flip chart. Averages are rounded to the nearest five where possible. The summary looks like:

Category	CEO	CFO	Retail	Ops	HR	Avg	Rnd
Sales	30%	20%	40%	20%	20%	26	25
Expense Control	10%	20%	10%	20%	20%	16	15
Productivity	10%	20%	10%	30%	30%	20	20
Cash Flow	10%	20%	10%	10%	---	10	10
Customer Satisfaction	20%	---	30%		10%	12	15
Reg. Compliance	---	---	---	10%	10%	4	---
Strategic Projects	20%	20%	---	10%	10%	12	15
Total = 100%	100%	100%	100%	100%	100%	100	100

STEP 3. The category balance is reviewed. The sums of the short-term vs. long-term measure category weightings are first compared. In the above example, the four short-term categories add up to 70%, while the two long-term categories total to 30%. The emphasis, then, is on short-term profitability. If this balance does not reflect the organization's strategy, the categories are re-weighted to provide a more accurate balance. Other balance issues to consider are sales vs. expense control, cash flow, customer satisfaction, and regulatory compliance;

and productivity vs. cash flow, customer satisfaction, regulatory compliance, and strategic projects.

STEP 4. The group then defines specific, quantifiable performance measures for each target category. In some cases, a category may be assigned more than one measure. When this occurs, the category weightings should be distributed among the measures to ensure the original category weightings remain the same. Below is a sample scorecard with specific measures.

Category	Weight	Measure 1	Measure 2
Sales	25	Current Sales (10)	New Sales (15)
Expense Control	15	Scrap / Revenue (15)	
Productivity	20	Labor / Revenue (20)	
Cash Flow	10	Past Due % (5)	Inventory Turns (5)
Customer Satisfaction	15	Survey (5)	Quality Roll-Up (10)
Strategic Projects	15	Project Roll-Up (15)	

STEP 5. A performance scorecard is designed for the above measures, including each measure's base (current, minimum) and goal. The sample strategic scorecard is presented below.

Category	Base	Goal	Weight
Current Sales	$10,000,000	$12,000,000	10%
New Sales	$3,000,000	$6,000,000	15%
Scrap / Revenue	6%	3%	15%
Labor / Revenue	28%	25%	20%
Past Due %	18%	10%	5%
Inventory Turns	2.2	3.2	5%
Avg. Survey Score	4.0	7.0	5%
Quality Roll-Up	0	100*	10%
Strategic Projects	0	100*	15%

* Note: The Quality Roll-Up and Strategic Projects are composite scores extracted from other scorecards. Composite scores are always assigned a base of zero and a goal of 100. The concepts of roll-ups and composite scores will be explained in detail in chapter nine.

Designing a Scorecard System 'Blueprint'

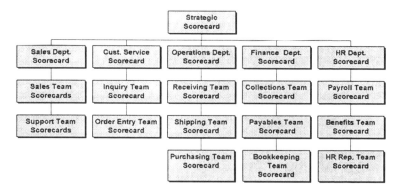

The method of cascading objectives begins with the design of the strategic scorecard. In the above example, this is followed by the design of departmental scorecards, then team scorecards. The number of cascades will depend upon the number of organizational levels, and how far down through the organization the scorecard system will be executed.

STEP 6. The organizational blueprint is a chart that is used to guide the cascading of the organizational scorecard measures down through the rest of the organization. The illustration below depicts this process. The blueprint is a table in which a column is provided for each strategic measure and a row for each job position in descending order. The following is an example of a blueprint for the organizational chart depicted above.

Sample Organizational Blueprint

Meas. Wght	Curr Sales 10%	New Sales 15%	Scrap /Rev. 15%	Labor /Rev. 20%	Past Due % 5%	Inven Turns 5%	Surv Score 5%	Qual 10%	Strat Proj 15%
Sales Dept.									
Sales									
Supp									
Cust Serv									
Inquiry									
Order Entry									
Operations									
Receiving									
Shipping									
Purchasing									
Fin-Ance									
Collections									
Payables									
Bookkeep									
HR									
Payroll									
Benefits									
HR Rep.									

STEP 7. The strategy planning group next assigns priority weights to each row in the blueprint. These weights should reflect the weights on the strategic scorecard, as much as possible. Some job positions will not relate to some strategic measures. In these cases, the weights will not match the strategic scorecard. However, the relative weights should be

similar – at least with respect to long-term vs. short term measures. The following is an example of how the assigned weights might look in the blueprint.

Measure Weight	Curr Sales 10%	New Sales 15%	Scrp /Rev. 15%	Labr/ Rev. * 20%	Past Due % 5%	Inv Turns 5%	Surv Scr 5%	Qual. 10%	Strat. Proj. 15%
Sales Dept.	30	40	--	--	10	10	10	--	--
Sales Team	35	45	--	--	--	10	10	--	--
Support Team	20	30	--	20	10	10	10		
Cust Serv Dept	20	--	--	20	--	10	20	10	20
Inquiry Team	20	--	--	20	--	10	30	20	--
Order Team	--	--	--	30	10	10	20	30	--
Operations Dept	5	10	20	30	--	5	5	10	15
Receiving Team	5	10	15	30	--	15	--	25	--
Shipping Team	5	10	15	30	--	10	10	20	--
Purchase Team	10	15	--	10	--	20	20	10	15
Finance Dept	--	15	--	40	25	--	10	10	--
Collect Team	5	10	--	20	35	--	10	20	--
Payables Team	--	--	--	50	--	20	--	30	
Bookkeep Team	--	--	--	50	10	--	10	30	
HR Dept	--	--	--	50	--	--	10	10	30
Payroll Team	--	--	--	80	--	--	10	10	--
Benefits Team	--	--	--	80	--	--	10	10	--
HR Rep. Team	--	--	--	65			10	10	15

* Note: The productivity measurement category includes internal customer quality and is thus high for support positions.

Assigning priority weights to each cascading job position is done before the measures are defined, for two reasons. First, this approach ensures the weights for each scorecard are aligned with the strategy. Second, the weights direct where the measurement effort will be focused. Cells on the blueprint with high weights should be assigned the most valid measures possible. Measures for the lower weight cells are less important.

Once the blueprint is completed, the next design phase is to assign specific measures to each targeted blueprint cell. These measures will be discussed in chapters 5-9. All measures will be reported monthly, using the scorecard format explained in chapter five.

Chapter 7

The Performance Scorecard

Over the past several years, a number of scorecard formats have been proposed. In our view, the most effective universal scorecard format was introduced in 1986 by Felix and Riggs at the University of Oregon Productivity Center. They termed their format the 'Performance Matrix.' We have successfully applied this measurement format across all types of industries and jobs, over the past 15 years, and find it to be flexible – and yet an excellent vehicle for ensuring balanced measurement.

The performance scorecard (matrix) has several unique and important features which ensure its ability to provide a universal measurement approach, balance performance, and align performance with strategy.

Performance Scorecard

Measures	\-20	\-10	0	10	20	30	40	50	60	80	100	WGT	WGT SCR
					Performance Scales								
Gross Revenue	10K	15K	20K	25K	30K	35K	40K	45K	50K	55K	60K	.20	\- 4
GP Margin %	9.0	9.5	10	10.5	11.0	11.5	12.0	12.5	13.0	13.5	14.0	.20	0
%Project Milestone	50	55	60	65	70	75	80	85	90	95	100	.40	20
Customer Survey	4.0	4.5	5.0	5.5	6.0	6.5	7.0	7.5	8.0	8.5	9.0	.20	20
			BASE							GOAL		36

Universal Approach

The scorecard provides interval look-up scales eliminating calculations that could prove difficult for some employees. Employees simply find the interval within which their performance falls, and look to the top of the scorecard to find the equivalent score. Alternatively, an organization could choose to compute the scores using the percent-gain formula **(actual − base) / (goal − base)**. The scorecard format can be applied to any type of measure that can be expressed as an ordinal number (dollars, percentages, ratings, etc.). Furthermore, any number of measures can be applied to the scorecard, although two-to-seven are recommended.

Balance Performances

- The scorecard converts all measure data to a common 'conversion' scale which is located at the top of the scorecard. These converted scores are multiplied by their priority weightings, and then summed to provide an overall score or performance index for the combined performances.

- A 'percent gain' between a 'base' and a 'goal' is computed, rather than a simple 'percent goal' or 'percent over base.' Anchoring both low and high performances allows a scale to be created which can then convert dissimilar measures to common scores.

- Each measure scale is 'capped' at both ends. This ensures balance, by not allowing extreme performances either above goal, or below base, to mask the true overall performance. (Methods for rewarding sales over goal will be described in the sales measurement chapter.)

Align Measures with Strategy

- The scorecard measure weights allow the designer to align each scorecard's priorities with the organization's strategic objectives priorities.

- The universal format of the scorecard facilitates organization-wide design and adminstration of the perfomance system. This ensures that all scorecards are aligned with the organization's objectives, and that incentive payouts are equitable and cost-effective across all job positions.

Components of the Scorecard

1) Performance Measures.

Number of Measures. Two-to-seven measures are recommended. The scorecard should have at least two measures, since most performances have counterbalancing consequences. Measures should not duplicate other measures (for example, sales and gross profit are closely related). Typically, the number of scorecard measures decreases as you cascade to lower levels of the organization.

Sub-Scorecards. Multiple performances can be weighted and measured on a sub-scorecard. The performance score of the sub-scorecard is then linked into the the main scorecard. For example, a salesperson may have several product sales goals which can be listed on a sub-scorecard. The weighted sum can then be linked to the salesperson's main scorecard, which may have collections, service, or other non-sales measures. Or, a team may have several projects assigned to them. These projects, and their milestone goals, can be listed on a sub-scorecard, and linked to the team's main scorecard.

Diagnostic Measures. It may be desirable to list some measures on a scorecard for purely infomational purposes. This can be accomplished by simply weighting the measure zero. The performance is tracked, but does not impact the scorecard performance index. Linked measures, sub-scorecards and diagnostic measures will be discussed in more detail in chapter nine.

Measures	-20	-10	0	10	20	30	40	50	60	80	100	WGT	WGT SCR
Gross Revenue	10K	15K	20K	25K	30K	35K	40K	45K	50K	55K	60K	.20	-4
GP Margin %	9.0	9.5	10	10.5	11.0	11.5	12.0	12.5	13.0	13.5	14.0	.20	0
%Project Milestone	50	55	60	65	70	75	80	85	90	95	100	.40	20
Customer Survey	4.0	4.5	5.0	5.5	6.0	6.5	7.0	7.5	8.0	8.5	9.0	.20	20

Performance Scales. BASE ... GOAL ... 36

Scale End-Points. The illustrated scale has end-points of –20 to 100. Any end-point values may be selected. However, it is recommended that the end-points should be the same for all scorecards in a performance system. Otherwise, scores across job positions will not be comparable, and incentive payouts will be inequitable. The –20 end-point subtracts points for performance below the 'base' level of performance. The purpose here, is to prevent employees from ignoring a measure and allowing performance to decline, while simply focusing on a few preferred measures. Technically, a perfectly balanced scale would range from –100 to 100. However, experience finds that the –20 is sufficient to prevent 'selective inattention'. More severe negative end-points appear to be overly punitive, and create too much unpredictability for the employee.

The upper end-point (goal) in the sample scorecard is 100. It is possible to set the endpoint at 120 or 130 which would represent 'stretch' goals, or performance above goal. This is a problem when the scorecard is used for incentive pay, since the incentive opportunity would be 130% rather than 100% (although adjustments could be made in the incentive opportunity amount to compensate).

Scale Intervals. There are eleven intervals on the sample scorecard's conversion scale. The number of intervals is somewhat arbitrary. Pragmatically, a large number of intervals makes automated reports difficult to format, while a small number of intervals is insensitive to incremental performance improvements. Performances that fall within an interval are rounded down. That is, performance is considered to be within an interval until performance reaches the next interval.

For example, if the 10 interval ranged from 0 to 5, a score of 4 would be converted to a 10 rather than the next highest interval. A common employee issue has been that scores near the next highest interval are still assigned that interval's conversion score. However, other approaches to rounding would simply shift the scale up proportionately since the base and goal would have to be adjusted.

Measures	Performance Scales										WGT	WGT SCR
	-20	-10	0	10	20	30	40	50	60	80	100	
Gross Revenue	10K	15K	20K	25K	30K	35K	40K	45K	50K	55K	60K	.20	-4
GP Margin %	9.0	9.5	10	10.5	11.0	11.5	12.0	12.5	13.0	13.5	14.0	.20	0
%Project Milestone	50	55	60	65	70	75	80	85	90	95	100	.40	20
Customer Survey	4.0	4.5	5.0	5.5	6.0	6.5	7.0	7.5	8.0	8.5	9.0	.20	20

BASE   GOAL   36

Accelerating Intervals. Note that on the sample scorecard the last two intervals increase at twice the amount as the earlier intervals. The notion here, is that incremental improvement becomes more difficult as you approach goal, and therefore score gains and incentive payouts should increase at a higher level near the goal.

Alternative Conversion Scales.

The conversion scale in the prior examples is an eleven-point interval scale of –20, –10, 0, 10, 20, 30, 40, 50, 60, 80, 100. Similar to the original Oregon Productivity Center scale, the scale includes two negative intervals to better balance performances. Further, the scale accelerates in the last two intervals to reinforce typically more difficult improvements near goal. Any scale, with any number of intervals, may be applied. Or, using the percent gain formula (actual – base / goal – base) a continuous scale can replace the interval scale.

There are two, 11-interval conversion scales that are common alternatives to the -20 – 100 scale. The first eliminates the negative intervals as well as the accelerating intervals near goal. This scale is preferred by some organizations because it is thought the negative intervals are demotivating, and the accelerating intervals complicate the scale. The second scale ranges from 30 to 130. The concept behind this scale is that the 100 interval will represent plan, or goal, while the intervals above 100 represent above goal or, 'stretch' performance.

Alternative 1: Linear Conversion Scale

Measures	Performance Scales											WGT	WGT SCR
	0	10	20	30	40	50	60	70	80	90	100		
Gross Revenue	10K	15K	20K	25K	30K	35K	40K	45K	50K	55K	60K	.20	- 4
GP Margin %	9.0	9.5	10	10.5	11.0	11.5	12.0	12.5	13.0	13.5	14.0	.20	0
%Project Milestone	50	55	60	65	70	75	80	85	90	95	100	.40	20
Customer Survey	4.0	4.5	5.0	5.5	6.0	6.5	7.0	7.5	8.0	8.5	9.0	.20	20

BASE   GOAL | 36 |

Alternative 2: Conversion Scale with 'Stretch' Intervals

Measures	Performance Scales											WGT	WGT SCR
	30	40	50	60	70	80	90	100	110	120	130		
Gross Revenue	10K	15K	20K	25K	30K	35K	40K	45K	50K	55K	60K	.20	- 4
GP Margin %	9.0	9.5	10	10.5	11.0	11.5	12.0	12.5	13.0	13.5	14.0	.20	0
%Project Milestone	50	55	60	65	70	75	80	85	90	95	100	.40	20
Customer Survey	4.0	4.5	5.0	5.5	6.0	6.5	7.0	7.5	8.0	8.5	9.0	.20	20

BASE   GOAL | 36 |

3) **Priority Weights.**

Priority weights can be adjusted at any time to reflect changes in strategy and tactics. The priority weight of a measure should be aligned with the priority weights of the strategic scorecard. It is suggested that, where possible, priority weights be assigned in increments of five to make the scorecard easier to interpret. A priority weighting of zero will display a measure in a scorecard, but the measure will not affect the overall performance index.

Measures	\multicolumn{12}{c}{Performance Scales}

Measures	-20	-10	0	10	20	30	40	50	60	80	100	WGT	WGT SCR
Gross Revenue	10K	15K	20K	25K	30K	35K	40K	45K	50K	55K	60K	.20	-4
GP Margin %	9.0	9.5	10	10.5	11.0	11.5	12.0	12.5	13.0	13.5	14.0	.20	0
%Project Milestone	50	55	60	65	70	75	80	85	90	95	100	.40	20
Customer Survey	4.0	4.5	5.0	5.5	6.0	6.5	7.0	7.5	8.0	8.5	9.0	.20	20

BASE   GOAL   36

Priority weightings normally sum to 100%. However, 'extra credit' can be assigned to a measure by weighting it such that the total weights sum to a number greater than 100%. Capping the performance index at 100% would prevent the total index from exceeding 100%, but still provide extra credit for a measure without exceeding the predefined incentive opportunity.

A negative priority weighting could be applied to a measure such that as performance reached 100%, the score would be subtracted from the total. Generally, this approach is not recommended, as it makes the scorecard more complicated to interpret.

Priority weightings can be assigned to 'mimic' existing conventional sales commission plans. Working backwards, the current commission earnings can be used to compute current commissions as a percentage of base salary. A weighting can then be constructed that parallels the payouts offered by the existing commission plan.

4) **Base and Goal.**

The base and goal must be defined before a performance measure's scale can be constructed. The base is defined as current or minimally acceptable performance, whichever is better. If the base is set too far above current performance, employees may be demotivated. The base is a management tool that should be applied from a behavioral perspective, rather than only a strategic perspective.

In contrast, the goal should be applied from a strategic perspective, with the exception of behavioral or process measures designed to 'jump-start' some missing employee behavior. The goal setting procedure varies with the type of measure.

Measures	\-20	\-10	0	10	20	30	40	50	60	80	100	WGT	WGT SCR
Gross Revenue	10K	15K	20K	25K	30K	35K	40K	45K	50K	55K	60K	20	-4
GP Margin %	9.0	9.5	10	10.5	11.0	11.5	12.0	12.5	13.0	13.5	14.0	20	0
%Project Milestone	50	55	60	65	70	75	80	85	90	95	100	40	20
Customer Survey	4.0	4.5	5.0	5.5	6.0	6.5	7.0	7.5	8.0	8.5	9.0	20	20

Performance Scales — BASE ... GOAL — 36

Goal Setting.

Budgeted. Goals can be established through the normal budgeting process. Revenue and expense goals are allocated down from the organizational level, such that they sum to the organizational goals. It may or may not, be a good practice to use the conventional budget numbers, depending upon the philosophy and methodology used to arrive at the budget.

Maximum Incentive Opportunity. Revenue and expense goals can be defined that produce a net income sufficient to fund the incentive plan at its maximum.

Improvement over previous year or previous three-year average.

Statistical definitions, such as one standard deviation above the mean, or the average of the top 15% of the baseline months.

Finanicial Ratios and Percentages.

If the measure is a financial ratio, the same procedures as above can be applied to the ratio numerator and denominator to compute the goal ratio.

Non-Financial Ratios.

For percentages that cannot exceed 100%, such as accuracy, on-time performance, etc., a base of 50 and a goal of 100 are good start points. If it is simply not possible to achieve 100 due to outside, uncontrollable factors then a goal less than 100 should be assigned.

Ratings.

The initial base and goal for survey ratings should be set at the rating scale average and maximum. If sufficient historical data exists, a mean and standard deviation can be used.

Special Cases. Often, there are extenuating circumstances that must be taken into account in the base- and goal-setting process. The following decision trees list special issues to consider when determining the base or goal.

Goal-Setting Decision Tree

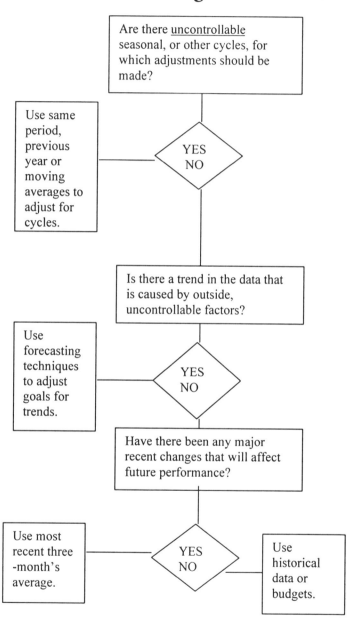

5) Performance Scales.

Once a measure's base and goal are defined, the remaining scale values are interpolated between the base and goal. Simply count the number of intervals between the base and goal, and divide into the difference between the base and goal. Then round to even numbers, if practical. For example, in the case of the sample scorecard measure 'gross revenue', the base is 20,000 and the goal is 60,000. The difference is 40,000. The number of intervals between the base and goal is 8. Therefore, 40,000 / 8 = 5,000 – the interval will be 5,000. To compute the two negative columns, simply apply the same interval to the base i.e. 20,000 – 5,000 and 15,000 – 5,000.

Performance Scales

Measures	-20	-10	0	10	20	30	40	50	60	80	100	WGT	WGT SCR
Gross Revenue	10K	15K	20K	25K	30K	35K	40K	45K	50K	55K	60K	.20	4
GP Margin %	9.0	9.5	10	10.5	11.0	11.5	12.0	12.5	13.0	13.5	14.0	.20	0
% Project Milestone	50	55	60	65	70	75	80	85	90	95	100	.40	20
Customer Survey	4.0	4.5	5.0	5.5	6.0	6.5	7.0	7.5	8.0	8.5	9.0	.20	20

BASE   GOAL   36

4) Weighted Score.

The weighted score is computed by locating the interval the actual data falls in for each measure. The conversion score at the top of the column is then multiplied by the measure's priority weight to compute the weighted score. In the sample, the actual score is represented by a bar.

Meas	-20	-10	0	10	20	30	40	50	60	80	10	WT	WT SCR
Rev	<u>10</u>	15	20	25	30	35	40	45	50	55	60	.20	-4
Margin	9.0	9.5	<u>10</u>	10.	11.	11.	12.	12.	13.	13.	14.	.20	0
% Prj Ms	50	55	60	65	70	75	80	<u>85</u>	90	95	10	.40	20
Cust Serv	4.0	4.5	5.0	5.5	6.0	6.5	7.0	7.5	8.0	8.5	<u>9.0</u>	.20	20

Performance

BASE   GOAL

36

Chapter 8

Performance Measurement Principles

Chapters 7 through 9 discussed specific measures for each of the seven measurement categories. There are, however, some measurement principles that apply to all measures, and that should be considered each time a measure is developed. This chapter discusses these basic measurement principles. The basic measurement issues to be discussed are: results vs. process measures, subjective vs. objective measures, group size, composite measures, and performance opportunity adjustments.

The Ten Commandments of Performance Measurement

I. No one should design their own incentive plan.

The manager, or someone other than the individual receiving the incentive payments, should design the scorecard. This third party person can solicit input from those who will be assigned the scorecard, but should not negotiate the measures or goals. Otherwise, the participants will be put in a self-serving position which may prejudice the design. The employees in the job are often too close to the work, and tend to design measures around processes and activities, rather than true results. In the design of incentive plans, management should think of itself as the "customer" and the participants as the "vendors." The customer always specifies what he wants and what he is willing to pay for it.

II. The frequency of measurement feedback is as important as the amount.

The more frequently measures can be reported, the more effective the measures will be in guiding behavior. Try to implement measures that, at a minimum, provide monthly feedback.

III.   Design ideal measures, then compromise.

Determine the strategic results of a job position and the key performance dimensions (productivity, quality, sales, etc.). Design the scorecard to improve these results without regard to what data are available. Then capture the data or compromise. Don't design the scorecard exclusively to what data are currently available.

IV.   The performance measures should "mirror" the real world.

Try to design scorecard measures as though the participants are franchised or in business for themselves.

V.   Where possible, design measures for small teams and individuals rather than large groups.

Individual measures have more impact on performance, are more equitable, and can more readily convert to leveraged incentive pay. Team measures may be combined with individual measures on the same scorecard, where appropriate.

VI.   Measure only controllable job outputs.

Design measures that are largely under the control of the participants. Do not use broad, financial or subjective measures affected by events the performer can't control.

VII.   Balance quality and quantity.

Never design one-dimensional scorecards that focus only on work quantity or quality. Make sure the two dimensions are balanced in terms of the economic consequences and the impact on long-term objectives.

VIII. Design "linked" measures to encourage employees in interdependent jobs to cooperate.

When the performance of one employee group consistently affects another employee group, you can improve cooperation by including one or more scorecard measures from group A's plan in group B's.

IX. Provide equity of opportunity, but not necessarily equity of result.

All participants should have an equal opportunity to achieve goals, but not necessarily every employee, nor every month. Employees should never come to see goal achievement as guaranteed, or an entitlement.

X. Try it, then fix it.

All the variables that may affect performance will only surface after installation. Scorecards should be piloted using non-monetary recognition, or low payout opportunity "capped" cash plans. Once you test the plans, and make adjustments, increase or remove the incentive caps.

Result vs. Process Measures

Ideally, every measure in a performance system would be a result measure. That is, it could be directly, and often mathematically, related to the organizational strategy and financial performance. This would ensure alignment and guarantee the validity of each measure. Unfortunately, there are many situations in which result measures are unsatisfactory. Process measures are either sub-components of a result, or the employee behaviors which drive a result. Because process measures are usually more closely under the control of employees, there are situations in which they are more effective than results measures. Below are some examples of results measures and possibly related process measures.

Result	Process
Revenue	Sales prospects seen, percent prospects closed, product cross-sell ratio, product up-sell (revenue per product)
Expenses	Equipment maintenance checklist, cycle count accuracy, production process checklist
Labor Expense	Productivity; efficiency, utilization, rework, internal quality
Accidents	Safety checklist, safety audit
Customer Attrition	Customer service rating, error rates, on-time delivery
Project Completion	Project milestones

Process measures should be considered whenever there are a large number of new or untrained employees; when there are high-impact, extraneous variables that affect the result; or when there is a long delay between the process and the result.

New or Untrained Employees. It is well established that training is most effective when followed by immediate on-the-job application of the training combined with precision behavior feedback and reinforcement. For example, a retail store decides to send its sales associates through a sales program. A significant part of the training relates to suggestive selling to customers at the counter. The sales trainer knows that only one-in-ten suggestions is every successful. Most associates are uncomfortable selling and would prefer to ignore the training. Measuring actual sales will not assist them in learning which suggestions are successful, under which conditions, and given what personal style. If the store elects to measure and pay incentives on actual monthly sales, the selling behaviors learned will likely not occur for most associates. There simply is too long a delay between the suggestion, the feedback, and the reinforcement. The number of suggestions made each day and the number of successful suggestions are process measures that will yield much better results.

One approach to process vs. results is to measure both, but initially weight the process measure higher on the scorecard. In the example above, we could measure suggestions and assign it a high weight, but also monthly sales with a low weight. Over time, the weights could be reversed as employees gain experience and are more successful.

Process Deficiency Clearly Identified. It may be that a result measure is not improving and the process cause is well known. For example, shipments may be late because orders are not submitted to the shipping department by the end of the previous day. To improve shipping results, we might measure the percentage of orders submitted to shipping by the end of day.

High Impact Extraneous Variables. Extraneous variables could arise from vendors, other departments, managers, or customers. For example, scrap rates could vary directly with the quality of raw materials supplied by the vendor. If this were a consistent, and irresolvable issue, a production process checklist might be added. If the correct process is used, then the goal is considered met. Other departments could send work downstream too late for the downstream unit to meet its deadline goals. A thruput, or turnaround measure, could replace, or augment the deadline goal. Turnaround measures the time interval between receipt of the input and the output time, and is therefore unaffected by late input.

Managers may need to frequently assign employees to unmeasured tasks, which would reduce their productivity and timeliness. A solution is to measure efficiency rather than productivity. Efficiency is defined as units produced divided by 'time in production.' Since time in production rather than actual hours is the denominator, off-task assignments have no effect on efficiency.

Customers may change their requirements without proper notification, resulting in missed deadlines and other problems. One solution, is to compare shipping performance to the original shipping date, rather than the adjusted one.

Delayed Results. Job positions that involve numerous projects, often have long delays between the processes and behaviors and the results. For example, marketing may have a long delay between the marketing effort and actual new sales. Computer programmers may have long delays between their behaviors and the final program and so on. In these instances, projects may need to be segmented into project milestones that can be accomplished within a month or less (the shorter the milestone durations the more effective the measure). Achieving the milestones on time would be measured rather than the final result.

Caution. Employees will almost always prefer process measures over results measures, because they are more under their direct control and less subject to extraneous variables. Often, however, choosing process measures over results measures simply masks the real problems rather than motivating employees to solve them. When it is unclear whether employees can influence a result, a result measure should always be implemented first. Process measures should only be applied when performance constraints are not alterable by employees or their managers.

Subjective vs. Objective Measurement

Subjective measures refer to manager, or other employee perceptions, of an employee's performance. Statements about employee attitudes and behaviors are rated by the manager and sometimes peers. There are three problems with this approach to performance measurement; rater bias, direction and feedback, and delay. Rater bias has been highly investigated, and it is well established that ratings are influenced by non-performance issues such as the employee's gender, race, age, appearance, social skills, social class and other non-performance characteristics. The 'likeability' of the employee is generalized, resulting in what is termed the 'halo' effect (people we like are seen as good performers), or the 'devil' effect (people we don't like are seen as poor performers). A related problem is that most managers do not trust ratings either, or are concerned about the social or legal implications of a poor rating. As a result, 'rating compression' tends to occur in which employees receive very similar ratings, regardless of actual performance.

Subjective ratings are not only inaccurate, they are a poor substitute for effective performance maangement. Ratings fail to provide specific objectives and goals (direction) for employees. Further, ratings provide ineffective feedback because they are often inaccurate and fail to identify specific performances that need improvement. A poor rating on "professionalism" does not pinpoint what needs to be accomplished. Managing employees through subjective performance reviews, forces employees to focus on the manager, rather than the job or the customer. The employee is subservient to manager perceptions and, cannot be truly empowered to work more independently.

Finally, subjective ratings are most commonly applied in the conventional 'annual performance review.' The practice of annual reviews runs contrary to good performance management, in that the performance feedback is much too delayed to be valuable in guiding or correcting performances during the year. Further, annual reviews attempt the near impossible task of summarizing performances over some 250 work days. Human performance is dynamic, and no single annual rating does much to accurately describe performance cycles and trends throughout an entire year.

Objective, quantifiable measures are, then, always preferable to subjective ratings with one notable exception. Customer and employee satisfaction are based upon subjective perceptions, and are therefore best measured through survey ratings. How a customer perceives an organization's service may in fact, be more important than actual, objective service levels.

Group Size

Group size refers to the number of employees assigned to the same scorecard measure and data. For example, profit-sharing measures the organizational net income to determine incentive pay distributions. The group size is, then, the number of employees in the organization. As measures move from the organizational level to division, department, team and individuals, the group size tends to diminish to a 'group' of one at the individual level. The following research on the effects of group size is taken from a study by the author which was published in *Organizational Change*, Context Press, Reno, 1999.

A study was conducted of 2,195 performance measures in organizations that included manufacturing, banking, publishing, retail, and distribution. Total employee groups ranged from 62 employees to 1,140. The number of employees assigned to the scorecard measure was compared to the measure's performance trend. The chart below summarizes the study results. All data were converted to standard scores to allow for comparisons. Therefore, zero on the vertical axis represents the average trend of all the measures. As the chart illustrates, when group size exceeds twelve employees, performance trends decline rapidly. When the chart is extended to group sizes beyond 50 employees, performance trends decline to zero.

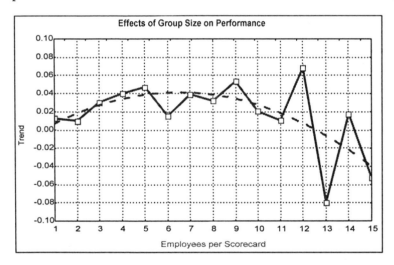

A second analysis was performed on the same data, in which the performance trends of scorecard measures assigned to only one employee (individual) were compared to scorecard measures that were assigned to two or more employees. The chart below illustrates the average trend of individual measures vs. team or group measures. As is evident, individual measures produce much higher improvement trends than do group measures.

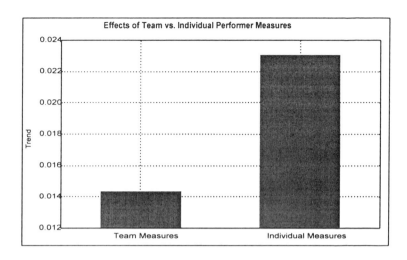

It is clear that measures should be assigned to small teams and individuals to optimize performance gains and, when used in an incentive pay program, to ensure equity by more precisely distributing profits to those who contribute the most. However, small team and individual measurement requires a lot of data. Further, such measures are often not found in existing databases. The trade-off is optimal performance and pay equity vs. difficulty of system administration. Some compromises are possible. For example, team and personal measures can be applied to critical job functions, while higher level measures are applied elsewhere. Or, team and personal measures can be applied only to measures that drive high priority strategic goals.

Composite Measures.

Composite measures include two or more performance dimensions in one measure. For example, net income can be measured, rather than measuring income and expenses separately. Other examples are total revenue, total expenses, standard hours, and net productivity (units – errors) / hours. Composite measures help ensure balance and empower employees to select which elements of the measure on which to focus their improvement efforts. However, composite measures do not allow the designer, or the manager, to prioritize specific performance elements of the measure, nor to analyze these elements independently. Generally, the greater the number of elements in a composite measure, the less immediate the performance improvement, due to the lack of employee focus created by several elements.

One tactic would be to implement composite measures and move to elements only if performance improvements fail to occur. Alternatively, an organization might begin with element measures and, as it seeks to empower employees, gradually transition to composite measures.

Performance Opportunity Adjustment.

Outside factors often affect an employee's ability to perform. A salesperson may have no prospects, or be short of product. A production employee has insufficient or poor quality input. Employees are assigned projects or meetings which take them off task. A lack of cooperation from vendors or other areas reduces performance. Customers buy seasonally, prices change, and equipment fails. The issue facing the designer is whether, and how, these outside factors should be adjusted for in the definition of a performance measure.

For example, a sales performance measure is designed for inside sales employees. One approach would be to simply measure the total revenue generated by each inside salesperson. However, it is argued that inside salespeople do not control the number of customer inquiries. Consequently, revenue per inquiry is selected as a measure to adjust for incoming inquiry volume. Choosing a ratio, filters out the effects of variations in inquiry volume. The employee is measured only on how effectively she generates revenue from each sales opportunity.

Further examination also finds that the inside salespeople are specialized in the products they sell. Inquiries are routed by the operator to the appropriate specialist. Some product lines sell at much higher prices than others. Therefore, sales per inquiry is biased in favor of those specialists offering higher priced products. The solution chosen, is to set different revenue / inquiry goals for each specialty line.

Two performance opportunity adjustments for inside sales have been made; measuring sales as a ratio and product line goal adjustments. The measurement is viewed by the employees as more fair than the original revenue per month. However, the complexity of the measurement system has increased substantially. There are also some potential flaws in the proposed measures. Mathematically, a salesperson could handle one inquiry a day and achieve the sales / customer goal. The fact that inquiry volume has been filltered out, could have an adverse impact on employee productivity. Further, the specialty goals were established using historical sales data. But are higher revenues per inquiry due to the products, or due to the historical performance of the employees in the speciality line? By setting different goals, have we made the system fair, or have we simply punished employees who performed well in the past?

Another major issue is whether or not we want empowered, proactive employees. We could allow the inside salespeople to telemarket, which would eliminate the need for a ratio. We could allow them to cross-train on other product lines to eliminate the specialty price issue and also to improve the consistency of inquiry volume. This would eliminate the need for specialty goals.

I once designed a performance measurement system for a medical lab typing pool. The team productivity measure was simply total analyses typed minus returned analyses. There was no adjustment for input volume. The team found this measure patently unfair. There were weeks when there simply were not enough analyses submitted to the department to meet the weekly production goal. A few months later, the department had solved the input problem by contracting with several client hospitals to handle some of their typing needs. As a result, the department achieved its weekly goal almost every week and became a revenue center for the laboratory!

One means for determining how empowered an employee group is, would be to examine the percentage of performance measures that are opportunity adjusted. The higher this percentage, the lower the empowerment. If an organization chooses to install measures that are not adjusted for opportunity, then it must truly empower employees to enable them to solve opportunity issues. Some organizations, neither adjust for opportunity, nor do they empower employees to solve opportunity problems. Employees correctly see this practice as unfair, and the results of the performance system are usually mediocre.

Situations exist in which employee empowerment cannot resolve the opportunity issue. In these cases, opportunity adjustments are required. In the sales example above, perhaps the nature of the business makes telemarketing undesirable or impossible. Perhaps the educational requirements to cross-train employees on other product lines are infeasible.

A major opportunity constraint for many employees is due to rapid and unpredictable changes in job responsibilities. Many employees attend meetings, training, coach other employees, work on projects, or are engaged in other activities that take time away from their assigned job results. The simplest solution is to assign higher level departmental, divisional, and organizational performance measures to these employees. The argument is that all their varied assignments can only be assessed at these levels. Unfortunately, the higher the measure level, the less personal control over the outcome. A second approach is to subtract off-task time from the productivity ratio denominator. A third strategy is to implement a 'credit' measurement system. That is, the productivity ratio numerator is increased by participating in off-task assignments. Additional measures could also be implemented for employees who spend a good deal of time training other employees or other activities. All of these measurement strategies involve some administrative overhead.

Three common opportunity adjustments to performance measures are ratios, percentages, and moving averages. Below are examples for each of the seven measurement categories.

Measure Category	Ratio	Percentage	Moving Average
Sales	Sales/Cust.	% Sales Goal	3 mma
Expense Control	Cost/Unit	% Budget	3 mma
Productivity	Labor/Unit	% Budget	3 mma
Cash Flow		% Past Dues Goal	YTD or 3 mma
Regulatory Compliance	Accidents / Hrs	% Wrk Comp Goal	3, 6, or 12 mma
Customer Satisfaction	Complaints / Ord	% Cust attrition Goal	3, 6, or 12 mma
Strategic Projects	% Milestones Met		YTD, 3, 6 or 12 mma

Linked Performance Measures

Linked measures are measures in which the data are reported in one scorecard, then imported or linked to another scorecard. Linked measures are mostly used to promote support and cooperation between two or more job positions.

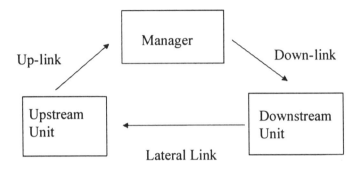

There are three major types of linked performance measures; up-links, down-links, and lateral links.

Up-Link. These links are also called 'roll-ups' and refer to employee performances that are exported to a manager or other higher level scorecard.

Down-Link. These links typically involve measuring support people (secretaries, administrative assistants or trainers) on the performance of the people they support.

Lateral-Link. These links refer to 'assembly-line' situations, in which one unit receives input from another. The upstream unit can be measured on the performance of the downstream unit.

Chapter 9

Performance Measurement: Sales

1) Outside Sales

Outside sales positions refer to salespeople who make in-person calls on prospects. The key behaviors include prospecting, closing, and cross and vertical selling. You may need to consider additional categories such as: customer service for sales staff who manage accounts; expense control where salespeople extend credit or travel substantially; and operational productivity where inappropriate sales orders can adversely affect manufacturing costs or delivery of the product or service.

Revenue vs. Gross Profit as a Sales Measure. Gross profit should be the sales measure of choice when salespeople have pricing or discount authority, or can significantly affect product mix and profitability by guiding customers toward particular products or services. Salespeople who have no such authorities, or effects on mix, can be measured on revenue rather than gross profit. To prevent holding orders, etc., and to increase monthly sales incentives, you may wish to consider a rolling, three-month average sales measure.

Sales Credits. You may prefer to consider sales "credits" as an alternative to revenue or gross profit. Sales credits are point values based on profitability that are assigned to products or product revenue dollars. The credit values may be based on any combination of marketing strategies, customer retention, manufacturing issues, or inventory reduction objectives. Multiply each sale or revenue dollar by its credit value and sum them to compute total sales credits. Sales credits give management more control over directing the sales mix, than do straight revenue or gross profit incentive plan measures. However, they are more difficult to administer and evaluate.

Sales/Selling Hour. For part-time salespeople, or employees who have other duties besides sales, it may be useful to measure sales per selling hour. Compute this by dividing total sales by selling hours for the month.

Prospecting. Prospecting is seeking out new customers. Although revenue or gross profit measures cover prospecting, you may wish to include a direct prospecting measure when: 1) you have a new sales force that needs a direct incentive for calling on prospects or; 2) you are concerned that salespeople will build up a territory and "sit on" the revenue from existing accounts thereby limiting your penetration of a market. Examples of prospecting measures are:

- The number of prospects seen each month
- The number of weighted prospects seen each month (weighted for potential value or contact difficulty)
- The percentage of an assigned prospect list seen

Selling Measures. Selling includes the closing of a prospect, the "cross-selling" of additional products and services, and the "vertical selling" of higher revenue or higher profit products and services. These measures may be included in your sales plan when you wish to emphasize a particular aspect of selling in managing your sales force. Alternatively, some or all, of these measures can be tracked for each salesperson for sales management, but not used to compute incentive payments. Examples of selling measures are:

Close Ratio. The number of prospects closed by the number seen. The close ratio is a useful sales management ratio, and may be desirable as a sales incentive measure where: 1) there is an emphasis on better qualifying prospects; or 2) salespeople may be wasting prospect leads through poor closing.

Cross-Sell Ratio. The cross-sell ratio refers to products or services sold to customers in addition to the basic product or service they purchased. Some industries refer to this type of sale as an "add-on" sale. The cross-sell ratio is computed as the number of products or services sold per customer. Cross-selling is a useful sales management measurement that you may wish to use as an incentive pay measure for outside salespeople when it is felt that cross-selling will: 1) improve the profitability per prospect, or 2) improve customer service and retention.

Vertical-Sell Ratio. The vertical-sell ratio refers to selling higher revenue, gross profit, or sales credit value products to customers. In some industries the ratio is also referred to as "upgrading" or "up-selling". To compute vertical sell, divide the total revenue, gross profit, or sales credits by the number of products or services sold in the month (revenue per product sold). Again, the vertical sell-ratio is a useful sales management measurement. You may wish to use the ratio as an incentive pay measure with outside salespeople when prospecting opportunities are limited and your goal is to increase the value of each customer relationship.

Sales Ratio. Cross-selling and vertical-selling can be combined into a single measure by dividing revenue, gross profit, or sales credits by the number of customers sold.

Sales Customer Service Measures. Where outside salespeople function as account representatives to a territory, it is essential that you consider account retention in the design of the sales incentive plan. One approach, used in many industries, is to measure the salesperson's on-going revenue, rather than simply the initial sale. This encourages the salesperson to remain concerned about the customer. Alternatively, you could add a customer service survey measure, or customer attrition measure, to the sales scorecard.

Linked Sales Measures. Many times, salespeople affect customer satisfaction by promising things that can't be delivered in a timely fashion or to specification. Such practices may not adversely affect the salesperson's incentive pay in a large territory, but can do serious damage to the organization by creating problems for production and customer service departments. If these are issues for your organization, two solutions are offered. Salespeople can be "linked" to on-time delivery measures in operations and order accuracy, or customer complaints in customer service. If these measures don't exist, an alternative (but less desirable) approach is to have these departments rate each salesperson on objective criteria and add this measure to the sales scorecard.

Less obvious, but sometimes substantial expense considerations, are the labor and material costs associated with sales promises that require undiscounted back-orders, or rush vendor and delivery freight expense. These expenses can again be "linked" to the sales plan, if they are tracked in purchasing and operations.

Sales Expense Measures. Where salespeople have significant control over travel, entertainment, advertising, or phone expense, it may be desirable to add a "travel and entertainment" measure to the scorecard.

A second type of expense is past due interest expense and charge-offs. These expenses are relevant when the salesperson has significant control over the granting of credit to customers. These expenses can be "linked" to the salesperson's scorecard, if they are measured in the credit and collections area.

SUMMARY OF POTENTIAL OUTSIDE SALES MEASURES

Sales Revenue	Revenue/month, YTD average revenue, rolling 3-month average revenue
Gross Profit	(same)
Sales Credits	Sum of revenue dollars or products x sales credit value
Sales/Hour	Revenue, gross profit, or sales credits divided by sales hours
Prospects Seen	The number of prospects seen per month
Wgt. Prospects	The sum of prospects seen multiplied by their priority weights
% List Seen	The number of assigned prospects seen, divided by the number of prospects assigned for the month
Close Ratio	The number of prospects sold, divided by the number of prospects seen
Cross-Sell Ratio	The number of products or services purchased, divided by the number of customers sold

Vertical-Sell Ratio	The revenue, gross profit, or sales credits per product sold
Sales Ratio	A combination of cross- and vertical-selling; the revenue, gross profit, or sales credits sold per customer
Cost of Sales	Travel, entertainment, advertising, phone expense over threshold subtracted directly from sales incentives or as a ratio to sales or sales incentives

"Linked Measures"

Customer Service	On-time delivery %, out of stock sales %, product return %, complaint %
Credit/Collections	% accounts past due 30 days, % charge-offs
Purchasing	% accounts sold that are out of stock or rush ordered
Operations	% on-time deliveries, labor + freight + materials expense /sales

NOTE: Linked measures may have to be applied to the sales team, rather than each individual salesperson depending upon data availability.

2) Inside Sales

Inside sales refers to salespeople who do not make outside sales calls. Though prospecting is a definite possibility through telemarketing, the measures described assume the salesperson has no control over customer traffic. They sit at a desk or counter and wait for customers to contact them.

Single Salesperson Departments. Given the reactive nature of inside sales, measures that rely on sales volumes such as revenue, gross profit, or sales credits per month are a problem. The total sales of an inside salesperson is mostly dependent upon advertising, store location, business cycles, and staffing. (The exception is that inside salespeople may be more eager to answer calls to increase sales volume.) The total sales may not accurately reflect the salesperson's performance, but more her opportunity to perform. A volume related measure will be quite demotivating to the inside salesperson in a slow month, since no amount of sales effort will enable the salesperson to achieve a significant incentive payment.

For a department with one inside salesperson, you must decide whether or not the customer traffic is stable enough to warrant a total sales per month measure. If not, you can increase the salesperson's consistency of opportunity by cross-training them in adjacent departments to provide them non-sales tasks that reduce their selling hours. In this case, sales per selling hour would be the scorecard measure. The employee can improve sales per selling hour, either by selling more to each customer, or by reducing selling hours through working on non-sales tasks.

Multiple Salesperson Departments. A second problem is that volume-driven sales measures may create competition in departments with two or more inside salespeople. This may create cooperation problems, and result in overly aggressive salespeople from the customer's perspective. One solution is to include a team measure.

Sales Ratios. Alternative solutions to inconsistent sales opportunity, or competitive situations, is to rely more on the sales ratio (sales per customer) or cross-sell ratio (products per customer) as a sales measure, rather than total sales. Vertical sales adds another behavioral dimension and encourages the salesperson to sell more high value products. Cross-sell has the advantage of most accurately reflecting the sales skills of the employee, in cases where vertical selling is unlikely.

Issues with Sales Ratios. When a sales ratio is used as the primary performance measure, two issues must be considered. First, the sales performance will not necessarily relate to the bottom-line results, since sales volume is not a consideration. For example, a sale of five products to one customer for the entire month would be computed as excellent sales performance, but would generate very little revenue. Second, our experience with sales ratios is that employees in departments with two salespeople may "shop" customers based on the likelihood they will purchase multiple products. A solution is to establish a customer count or total revenue scorecard measure to balance the ratio with the volume.

SUMMARY OF POTENTIAL INSIDE SALES MEASURES

Sales Revenue	Revenue / month
Gross Profit	(same)
Sales Credits	Sum of revenue dollars, or products x sales credit values
Sales / Hour	Revenue, gross profit, or credits, divided by sales hours
Cross-Sell Ratio	The number of products or services purchased, divided by the number of customers sold
Vertical-Sell Ratio	The revenue, gross profit, or sales credits per product sold
Sales Ratio	A combination of cross and vertical selling; the revenue, gross profit, or sales credits sold per customer

Chapter 10

Performance Measurement: Productivity and Expense Control

Productivity Measures.

Productivity is mathematically expressed as:

NET PRODUCTIVITY = EFFICIENCY x UTILIZATION x REWORK

Where:

EFFICIENCY = $\dfrac{\text{Production volume*}}{\text{Production time}}$

UTILIZATION = $\dfrac{\text{Production time}}{\text{Actual time}}$

REWORK = $\dfrac{\text{Production volume minus rework}}{\text{Production volume}}$

*Production volume must be converted to standard time for the formula. Standard time multiplies each unit of volume by the time it takes an average performer to process the unit.

For example, a data entry manager determines that each item requires an average operator 2 seconds to enter. The operator enters 6000 items to produce 2 x 6000 = 12,000 seconds which equals 200 minutes of "earned time." The operator spends four hours, or 240 minutes, processing this work, and is at work for eight actual hours (480 minutes). The operator makes 60 errors that must be corrected by others. The formula would be:

```
NET PRODUCTIVITY  = EFFICIENCY x UTIL x REWORK
     200 / 480=        200 / 240   240 / 480  (200 –2 / 200)
        41%               83%         50%          99%

              41%   = 83% x 50% x 99%
```

This operator would improve her productivity most by increasing her utilization from 50% of the day to 100%. However, if only 6,000 items are available for processing, this increase would simply halve the efficiency from 83% to 42%, with no effect on overall productivity. Put another way, the labor cost to process an item would remain the same. To ensure a true productivity improvement, the critical measure is "items per actual (time sheet) hour." That is, the number of items entered, divided by the actual time at work.

The problem with productivity as a measure, is that typically the data entry operator has no control over the amount of available work. Consequently, productivity (volume / actual hours) as a measure, includes a large uncontrollable component. On days with little work input, the operator will not be able to meet goal. There are three solutions to this problem.

Productivity is an often-misunderstood concept. I once received a call from an operations manager who complained his department's productivity measure was invalid. Productivity had improved substantially, and the employees were receiving incentive payments for the improvement. His complaint was that the number of employees, and the payroll expense, had not changed therefore there could not be a productivity improvement. Further discussion found that the input volume had almost doubled in the past several months. The department was still meeting its throughput goal with the same staff. The supervisor had focused only on the numerator of the productivity ratio, the payroll cost, while ignoring the denominator, the input volume.

1) **Efficiency Measure.** Instead of measuring productivity, an alternative measure would be the rate or efficiency (volume / time). The operator's supervisor signs the operator off-production during low input volume periods. To illustrate the difference in productivity vs. efficiency, suppose an operator produced four hours of errorless work (7,200 items x 2 seconds = 14,400 seconds divided by 3600 seconds = four hours of earned work) in four production hours over an eight-hour work day. The operator's productivity would be (4/8 = 50%). However, the operator's efficiency would be (4/4) = 100%. Using rate as the measure, the operator achieves goal, and is not penalized for the four hours of the day when no volume was available.

Though the efficiency measure is fair to the operator, its drawback is that an operator could work one hour a day, produce an hour's worth of work, and be paid the maximum incentive. The company's compensation expense increases without an increase in true productivity. Despite this problem, efficiency measures can be useful to the company. When the data entry department is trying to meet deadlines or has turnaround goals, efficiency measures encourages the operators to complete input volumes as fast as possible.

I once designed an incentive system in which the data entry operators were paid to improve their efficiency, while the supervisor was paid to improve operator utilization. After the program had been in effect for a while, the supervisor came to me with a complaint. It seemed that the more efficient the operators were, the lower the utilization and the less incentive pay earned by the supervisor. It immediately struck me that the plan was illogical. Given a constant input volume, the faster the operators entered data, the less time they were in production. A situation similar to the renowned Army slogan, 'hurry up and wait." The solutions were to measure the supervisor on productivity and to give her staffing authority.

2) Productivity Adjusted by Cross-Utilization. Productivity (volume / actual hours) can be made a more fair measure by cross-training the operator and subtracting time spent working in other areas as "off-production" time. In this variation, when the operator runs out of input volume, she is allowed to 'sign off' production hours when she moves to another job position. This encourages the operator to cross-train to reduce the denominator production hours in the productivity ratio. In our earlier example, the operator produced four hours worth of work in four production hours within an eight hour work day. In the adjusted plan, we assume the operator worked in another job position for two hours. The adjusted net rate would be four hours of work volume, divided by six hours of production (eight actual hours minus two hours in another job). The productivity percentage would then be 4 / 6 or 67%. This plan would encourage the operator to complete work input quickly and move to another job to reduce production hours.

3) Performance Scorecard. The performance scorecard provides the company with more targeted control over the three basic issues in data entry performance. Simply changing the priority weights of each performance measure (productivity, efficiency, and utilization) will focus the operators on a targeted dimension. The scorecard also allows the designer to include departmental measures for meeting deadlines in each individual operator's plan. The measures and priority weights for a production scorecard focused on increasing cross-training might be:

	Base	Goal	Weight
Accuracy	99.4%	100%	20% (volume-errors) volume
Rate	75%	100%	20% (volume-errors) prod hrs
Utilization	60%	90%	50% (prd+crs-ut hrs) actual hrs.

%Deadlines   90%   98%   10% # days dl met
                                                # work days

4) **Production Team Scorecards.** A team scorecard measures the performance of a group of employees who produce a common product or service. You would usually include the supervisor on the team. Each team member receives the same score, based on the overall team results. Typical team performance measures include:

Productivity Measures

Team Labor Hours Per Unit
Team Units Per Labor Hour
Team Weighted Units Per Labor Hour
Team Payroll Expense Per Unit

Labor hours may be actual, or actual minus "loaned" to other areas to promote cross-training.

Accuracy Measures

Team Error %
Team Accuracy %
Team Return %

Timeliness Measures

Team % Jobs Meeting Turnaround Goal
Team % Jobs Meeting Deadline
Team % Deadlines Met with all Jobs Completed
Team % Days in the Month all Jobs Completed by End of Day or Shift

In addition to accuracy and timeliness, you may wish to include an "internal" customer (other departments or teams), and/or an external customer service rating of the team.

Expense Measures

Team Supply, Maintenance, Scrap, Utility, Rework, Materials, Expense Per Unit

Administrative Measures

Team Attendance %
Team Safety Score
Team Housekeeping Score

5) Modifying Production Team Plans for Departmental or "Line" Performance. A potential difficulty with team plans on a production line is that some teams may perform well and receive incentive payments, but the overall result of the line or the department is not an improvement for the organization. This happens when several upstream teams meet their turnaround or accuracy goals, but later downstream teams do not. The result is the product or service is not produced on time, but some teams are paid incentives. A solution to this problem is to include total line or departmental performance measures in the team plans.

6) Modifying Production Team Plans for Personal Performance. A pure team plan does not recognize the individual contributions of the team members. This can create a perception of inequity among the team members, if some members contribute more than others. The solution may be to add one or more individual performance measures to the team plan. These individual measures may be personal production, personal error rate, personal attendance or a team contribution rating by the supervisor or team members.

Cash Flow Measures

General Cash Flow Formula

The general cash flow formula for days cash outstanding is useful for setting overall cash flow goals for the organization. The formula is:

Days Cash Out = Days Sales Out + Days Inventory Out − Days Payables Out

The organization can establish an overall 'days cash out' goal, and then prorate the goal to the three dimensions of cash flow using the above formula.

An alternative cash flow measure is the 'flow ratio' which is computed as:

$$\text{Flow Ratio} = \frac{\text{Total Current Assets - Cash}}{\text{Total Current Liability - Short-term debt}}$$

Collections (Days Sales Out)

The type of collector, to be discussed here, performs collection activities over the phone and through the mail. Collections plans are obviously related to the expense control category, but may also need to be linked to either sales or customer service department measures.

Behavioral Measures. Behavioral measures of collections include number of collection phone calls, phone contacts, and "promises to pay." My experience with these types of measures is that they promote activity but not much in the way of actual results. Such measures however, may be used in a scorecard, in addition to results, measures for collections performance management.

Results Measures. Results measures of collections include percent 30-, 60- or 90-day percent past due accounts or dollars; percent of accounts or dollars collected; average outstanding days of a collection dollar; and the charge-off percentage.

Percent Past Due. The percentage of past due accounts, or dollars in a collector's queue, at the end of the month. Typically, dollars past due is the preferred measure. However, where collections is seen more as a means of preventing charge offs, some companies prefer to use percent accounts.

Percent Collected. Computed as the number of past due accounts or dollars in the queue at the beginning of the month, divided into the number at the end of the month. This is a more accurate reflection of actual collection activity.

Average Outstanding Days of a Collection Dollar. Computed as the past due dollar amount of each account, multiplied by its past due days at the end of the month, divided by the total past due dollars in the queue. This measure is useful in that the "float" expense of uncollected funds can easily be computed, and used to determine the bottom-line value of collection activity. For example, a queue with three accounts would be computed as:

Account	Past Due $	Days Past Due	Weighted Days
1	$5,000	40	200,000
2	$8,000	30	240,000
3	$2,000	45	90,000
Totals	$15,000		530,000

Average weighted days past due = $530,000 / $15,000 = 35.3

Bottom-line results:

8% interest rate / 365 days = .000219 x 35.3 = .0077

.0077 x $15,000 = $116 interest cost on past due accounts

Charge-Off Percent. The percent of the queue accounts dollars that are charged off. Often, it is a second measure in the scorecard in addition to past dues.

Queue Size. Using any of the above results measures, collectors may be allowed to expand their queue sizes to increase their incentive opportunity. Since an increase in queue size requires more accounts to be collected to maintain the same collection percentage, the desire for a larger queue is counterbalanced by the increased difficulty in maintaining a low past due percentage. Increases in queue size may be an additional scorecard measure, or could increase the collector's incentive pay opportunity.

Linked Measures. Overly aggressive collection activity can cause the business to lose customers. It may be wise to add a linked measure from sales or customer service, such as the account retention percentage, customer survey score, or a complaint percentage.

Inventory Control (Days Inventory Out).

Inventory control measures include both cash flow, expense control and quality issues. Some common measures are:

Inventory Cash Flow Measures.

Days Inventory Outstanding. Conceptually, the number of days inventory remains in stock. Computed as 360 / Cost of Goods Sold / Inventory).

Inventory Turns. An alternative expression of DIO, computed by dividing cost of goods sold by inventory cost.

Inventory Expense Control Measures.

Purchasing Expense Control. In some cases, the purchase or discounted price can be compared to the retail price to compute a % of retail purchasing expense.

% Spoilage. The percent of inventory written off, due to product expiration.

% Shrinkage. The percent of inventory written off because it was lost or stolen.

Inventory Quality Measures.

Cycle Count Accuracy %. This measure relates to both cash flow and inventory quality. An inspection of a sample of the inventory is made, and the percentage of accurate inventory counts to total counts is computed.

% Backorders. A measure of the timeliness of inventory.

% Returns. A measure of the quality of inventory.

% Production Schedule Met. A linked measure of the timeliness of inventory, which assumes that inventory completeness directly affects the ability to meet production schedules.

% Shipping Dates Met. A linked measure of the timeliness of inventory, which assumes that inventory completeness directly affects the ability to meet shipping dates.

Express Shipping Expense / Revenue. Another measure of inventory timeliness, which is similar to backorders.

Customer Survey Responses. Survey responses can inquire as to customer perceptions of both the timeliness and quality of product or service received.

Payables (Days Payables Outstanding)

Payables measures include measures of timeliness, expense control, and product quality.

Payables Timeliness. The percent of payables made within the payables guidelines.

Payables Expense Control. The percent of payables in which discounts were taken.

Payables Quality. The percent of payables errors, or the results of a vendor survey.

Cash Flow Related Scorecards

Purchasing Manager/Staff

The purchasing function's performance dimensions may include sales, service, accuracy, timeliness, and expense control.

Linked Measures.

The purchasing agent affects customer satisfaction and retention by stocking items required by repeat customers. You may wish to link the purchasing agent to either sales, existing customer measures, or account retention measures.

The purchasing agent affects sales by ensuring products that would attract new customers are in stock, at the right price, and of high quality. To ensure the purchasing agent is concerned with sales, you may wish to link the sales department's performance (see sales plans) to the purchasing agent's plan.

Customer Survey. A customer survey that includes items concerning delivery timeliness, price, and product quality may be included in the purchasing agent plan.

% Orders with out-of-stock items. The percentage of orders written that are back ordered, substituted, or canceled due to an out-of-stock condition.

% Complaints. The number of customer complaints related to product price, or quality, divided by the number of orders filled in the month.

Accuracy and Timeliness Measures.

% returns due to wrong product in stock. The number of orders returned due to wrong product stocked.

% new stock on time, % back orders on time. The percentage of new stock, or back order requests, stocked within the goal turnaround time.

Cash Flow Measures.

% Inventory turn goal(s) met. The percentage of turn goals met or the percentage of stock meeting the turn goal.

Inventory interest expense as a percent of sales.

Warehouse Manager/Staff

A common warehouse position is the "picker" who may both put new stock into inventory and pick stock from inventory when it is to be shipped. The picker position's performance dimensions may be sales, accuracy, timeliness, service, productivity and expense control.

Sales Measures.

A sales measure applies when the picker, not only picks the item from inventory, but also comes in contact with customers either over the phone, as the order is placed, or at the counter when the order is picked up. In either case, there is a clear "cross-sell" opportunity. For example, if the customer orders a drill, drill bits could be suggested. If the customer orders cable, connectors could be suggested. This cross-selling not only increases revenue, but is viewed as good customer service.

To measure cross-sell over the phone, the percentage of orders sold with targeted cross-sell products could be measured. To measure over-the-counter cross-sell, the percentage of orders with additions to the invoice made at the counter could be measured.

Accuracy, Timeliness, and Service Measures.

Percent accurate picks. Depending upon the structure of your workflow, picking accuracy may be measured by the packers, inspectors, loaders, or drivers. If this isn't possible, then customer product-return rate must be used. If one or more of these job functions does exist, then these functions could measure the accuracy and timeliness of the picker.

Picking accuracy is measured as number of orders or items picked accurately. The formula would be (orders picked - orders rejected) / orders picked. Where the importance of accuracy is related to the item, a third possibility would be to measure the dollar value of the items picked. This formula would be (dollar value of items picked minus the dollar value of items rejected) divided by the dollar value of items picked.

Percent timely picks. Picking timeliness can be measured as a turnaround time or against delivery deadlines. Picking turnaround time would measure the average time between receipt of the picking order and completion of the order. A turnaround goal could also be established, and the percent orders picked within the goal turnaround time measured. Alternatively, the percentage of orders picked by deadline, or the percentage of days all orders picked by deadline, could be measured. This last measure is one of the simplest to manage. All picks are completed by 3:00 P.M. – yes or no. The number of work days in the month is divided into the number of days all orders were picked by 3:00, to compute the percent days all orders picked by deadline.

Service. The percent orders or items returned by customers, and the percent deliveries shipped on time, are the service measures of choice. However, it may be difficult to assign these measures to individual pickers or picker teams. In this case, a warehouse-wide measure would be computed and the score assigned to each individual picker or picker team.

Productivity Measures.

Percent days' picks completed by deadline. This measure is not a true productivity measure, since it fails to compare labor to volume. That is, the warehouse could simply hire twice as many pickers and always meet the deadline. However, assuming hiring decisions are outside the warehouse management's control, it is a simple measure to track that relates to productivity.

Picks per labor hour. This is a true productivity measure. Orders, or items, per labor hour is tracked. Where it is difficult to track this measure by individual picker, it can be made a team productivity measure. Because picking is often a cyclic activity, you may wish to encourage picker cross-training by subtracting hours from the productivity ratio's denominator, when pickers work in other job positions.

Expense Measures.

Key expense measures are damaged goods, supplies, freight costs and shrinkage. Supplies refer to the packing materials, where the picker is also the packer. Efficient packing cannot only reduce packing materials expense, but also delivery expense (smaller or fewer boxes) and customer returns due to damage in transit caused by poor packing. Delivery expense can be affected by reducing rush orders, optimizing truck loads, and reducing product return delivery expense. Shrinkage refers to lost or stolen goods. Typically, expenses are computed as a percentage of cost of goods, or sales per item, or per order. Expenses are generally tracked at the warehouse level, with the measure linked to each picker's or picker team's scorecard.

Expense Control Measures.

Expense control measures, as defined here, do not include labor expense, which has been categorized as 'productivity' and has its own unique measurements.

A common measurement practice is to measure expenses as a percentage of budget, or percentage expenses within a budget range, (ie. 95% of budget to 105% of budget). There are problems with percent of budget as a performance measure. First, the validity of the goal is greatly influenced by the person who creates the budget. Percent of budget may actually be more a measure of budgeting accuracy than expense control performance. Further, budgets are based on projected, rather than actual volumes. A more valid measure is the ratio of expenses compared to actual volume. Finally, budgets are designed for control more so than for performance improvement. From a control viewpoint, meeting the budget is the goal. From an improvement viewpoint, reducing expenses below budget may be the goal. As has been mentioned previously, performance measures should be influenced by employees. There is no logical reason to measure an employee on something he or she can't affect. Some examples of expense control measures are:

Travel and entertainment expense / sales or per sales call
Phone expense / phone calls, revenue or per employee
Return expense or warranty expense / revenue or per sale
Number of returns / number of orders or shipments
Maintenance expense / units produced or machine hours
Supply expense / revenue, units, or per employee
Scrap expense / materials expense or per unit produced
Purchasing expense / purchasing expense – available discounts
Recruiting, advertising and agency expense / hire
Marketing expense / revenue or number of prospects
Workman's compensation expense / payroll or number of employees
Overtime expense / regular payroll or O.T. hrs / regular hours

Any collection of these measures, that can be compared to a common denominator, can be combined to compute a 'controllable expense.' This combination reduces the number of measures tracked, and enables employees discretion in which expenses to target.

Chapter 11

Performance Measurement: Customer Service and Regulatory Compliance

Customer service is ususally the weakest component of an organization's measurement system. There are three main reasons for this neglect. First, the effects of changes in customer service are gradual and delayed. Many organizations react to service problems too late, and after the damage to the customer base may be irreversible. Second, at its roots, customer service is what customers *perceive it to be*, and therefore is less quantifiable than other measurement categories. What a customer perceives service quality to be, is ultimately more important than the actual service level. Third, customer service is often difficult to measure consistently. This is due to the typical delay between the employee behavior and the customer response and the fact that most service data do not exist in an organization's conventional reporting systems.

There are three categories of customer service measures: timeliness, quality, and 'style.' Timeliness measures include response time, turnaround time, and deadlines. Quality measures include accuracy and completeness. Style measures include cordiality, helpfulness, knowledge, and other such descriptions of employee behavior.

Objective Customer Service Measures

Objective service measures track actual performance on two of the three dimensions of service (they cannot track style). These measures are valuable, because they provide more immediate and concrete feedback regarding service levels than do survey data. They cannot, however, replace customer survey data, since service levels are subjective customer impressions. They are, however, useful for interpreting survey findings and in developing improvement plans.

Service Response Timeliness. Response time refers to the delay between a customer inquiry or request, and the organizations response. Examples are: the delay between a customer's arrival and an employee greeting; the delay between a phone inquiry and an employee answering the call; the delay between a request for service and the arrival of the technician or delivery person. Response time considers the delay in addressing a customer concern, rather than the time required to resolve the customer's concern. Response time is important because it is usually a customer's first impression of the organization.

There are two common measures of response time–the percent of responses occuring within a specified time period, or the average response time. If the company has researched what response time is required by its customers, the former measure provides better information. If there is no specific response time goal, the latter measure is the only option.

Percent calls meeting the response time goal is better information than the average, in that the average response time could improve due to a reduction in long delays, while in fact, the goal response time is never met. On the other hand, average response time provides better information on the frequency of these 'outliers' than does percent on-time. Average wait time is the inverse of average response time. In some situations it is easier to measure wait time than the response time itself.

The major drawback to response time service measurement, is that it is difficult to track effectively. Some time ago, we were asked to develop a response time measure for a bank's branch lobbies. Because I had began my college career in electrical engineering, I attempted to devise an electronic recording solution. The first attempt was to place a switch on the door, which activated when the door was opened (there is almost always only one entry to a bank branch for security reasons). By comparing entry times to exit times, we were able to determine the average customer time in the lobby.

Unfortunately, this simple solution proved ineffective, since customers sometimes opened, shut, and then reopened the door, or opened the door for someone else. These extraneous data invalidated the data for the day. Switches were then placed in floor mats just inside the door. This solution also failed, because people stepped on the mat multiple times. Finally I arrived at a solution. Infra-red beams were placed at the beginning of the branch wait line. Two beams were employed to adjust for customers moving backwards.

The data from these systems provided a daily graph of customer wait time. These data were then used to determine staffing levels throughout the day to ensure the wait-time goal was consistently met. As an aside, the average wait time for one branch increased dramatically in one of the months. Thinking I had found an improvement opportunity, I presented the finding to the branch's senior management. An inquiry found that the branch had been robbed that month and all the customers were laying on the floor for a half-hour!

For retail outlets, the manager can sample the number of customers in line during the day. Other means for collecting response time data are the time stamp, 'take a number' system, or time logs kept by employees. For example, the time a request for a service call is made, or a customer arrives for an appointment, can be logged on a computer. The technician or receptionist can then record the arrival or appointment time to compute the delay. This system produced remarkable results for a group of doctors' offices, where patient wait-time is a universal problem. A group incentive pay measure was based upon the average patient wait-time during the month (excluding the receptionist who was rewarded for the accuracy of the log).

Another approach to response time measurement is touch-screen technology. The customer enters a unique identification upon entering the business's premises, and again when served, or when leaving. Alternatively, the entry time can be compared to a log file recorded by employees, if it is not possible to get the customer to enter the i.d. when leaving. We have placed touch-screen systems in several retail and banking organizations with good success. The customer enters the i.d. and is asked to complete a brief customer satisfaction or marketing survey using the touch screen. To encourage and reinforce entering the i.d., we added a prize feature to the system. After completing the survey, the customer may elect to pick a 'lucky' number from a spinning display of numbers. If a prize is awarded, the system prints a receipt the customer can then exchange for a gift.

Telephone inquiry response time can be automatically monitored by most PBX systems as an additional, low-cost add-on. These systems variously track average time to pick-up, number of rings to pick-up, and number of abandoned calls. Given this technology, every organization should be monitoring telephone response time. With the advent of E-business, software is available that measures the number of web page hits and may be available for system response time as well.

Service/product turnaround timeliness.

Turnaround time refers to the delay between a request for a service or product, and receipt of the service or product. Generally, it is more easily measured than response time, since the request and delivery are usually logged in the normal business process. Turnaround measures are the same as response time, and include percent requests meeting the turnaround goal time, as well as the average turnaround time. Additional measures include percent out-of-stock, and percent backorders, for inventory-driven organizations.

Turnaround time is often influenced by extraneous variables including employee or product availability, the complexity of the request, required research, and others. For this reason it may be advisable to categorize turnaround requests and define unique goals for each category. This approach will require a coding system that allows the requests to be sorted into categories.

Service/product deadline timeliness.

Deadlines are, in some ways, the most critical type of timeliness measure. A deadline or delivery date is an explicit promise to a customer. In many cases the customer plans around the deadline. Failures to meet deadlines have serious implications. A very simple measure of deadline performance is the number of order cancellations. A more typical measure of deadline performance is the percent of deadlines met.

Though an acceptable measure, there are three problems with it. The percent deadlines met goal, can be achieved by an employee who simply quotes more delayed deadlines. Though the promise is kept, this practice may lose business when rapid fulfillment of the request is important to the customer.

When using deadline measures, management must be careful that the deadline is a real customer deadline. In our experience, deadline definitions are often changed by employees to the point they really mean the date the service or product was actually delivered. For example, a customer may have a deadline of September 15. However, the vendor has to back-order the product. The backorder delay is added to the original deadline to define a new deadline (even though the customer may not have been consulted). Where deadline performance is influenced by outside variables, the solution should be to lower the goal–not redefine the deadline.

When a product or service is delivered one day past the deadline, this may be a serious issue if the request was made the day before, but not as serious if the request was made several months before. To address this issue, a 'percent on-time' measure should be substituted for percent deadlines met. Percent on-time is computed as (deadline date - date initiated) / (date received - date initiated).

For example, two requests are made for products on the 10th of the month. The deadline for product A is the 20th of the month and it is received on the 22nd, while the deadline for product B is the 15th of the following month and it is received on the 17th of that month. Dates can be converted to Julian dates, or the total days or work days between initiation and the deadline/received dates can be computed.

The % on-time computations would be:

Product	Initiated	Received	Deadline	Days Late
A	10	22	20	2
B	10	37	35	2

% on-time for A = (20 – 10) / (22 – 10) = 10 / 12 = 83%

% on-time for B = (35 – 10) / (37 – 10) = 25 / 27 = 92%

A simple days-late measure would evaluate both products as having been delivered at the same level of quality. The % on-time measure would consider the deadline performance of product B better than A's.

Service and product quality.

A time-honored measure of quality is the number of customer complaints received each month. This measure is flawed by sampling problems with respect to what percentage of dissatisfied customers call, and whether they are typical of the total customer base. If complaints are used as a measure of customer satisfaction, they should be expressed as a ratio to total sales or total customers. I was in a meeting with a client group when the president burst in, upset that he had received 12 customer complaints this month, when he used to only receive five or six. He calmed down when he was reminded that the customer base had tripled over the past two years due to acquisitions. Given this, 15-18 complaints would not have been an increase–in fact, 12 was a decrease in the complaint rate.

Returns, recalls, rework, and warranty expense are reasonably easy-to-track measures of service and product quality. Generally, they should be expressed as a ratio to revenue, or number of services or products delivered. For simplicity, these events should be applied in the month they occur, rather than trying to apply them to the original order month.

Errors can be tracked internally by a quality assurance group before the customer receives the product or service. Typically, products or services are sampled. Sampling techniques are well established, but beyond the scope of this book. A caution however, is that customer service always refers to errors or delays the customer actually experiences. That is, internal organizational quality measures are valuable as analytical and preventative measures, but are not substitutes for external measures that reflect what the customer actually receives.

Customer Service Style. Service style (cordiality, helpfulness, knowledge) is often, more important than timeliness or quality. I have seen many situations where the product or service was on time and accurate, but the service employee so rude or unhelpful the customer account was terminated. On the other hand, a very cordial, helpful, and knowledgable employee can often maintain customer loyalty, even when the actual service levels are mediocre.

Unfortunately, objective measures of this dimension of service are difficult to obtain. To develop an objective measurement for style, the first step is to design a 'service model'. The model is a list of behaviors the employee is expected to perform. These statements should be specific, and should be stated in the past tense – as something done. For example, the statement "the employee is friendly" fails to describe specific results in the past tense. A better statement would be "the employee maintained eye contact" or the "employee smiled" or "the employee referred to the customer by name". Each behavioral statement should be tested for objectivity by having three independent observers view several service situations and check the behaviors which were performed. The observer scores will be the same if the list is truly objective.

Once the model is constructed, two methods can be used to apply the model. For telephone service, the service reviewer can randomly audit a sample of calls each month and complete the service checklist. Alternatively, some or all of the calls can be recorded and a sample of recorded calls can be played back for review. The recorded calls have the instructional advantage of allowing the reviewer to play back examples of an employee's good and bad service, or to collect samples of good and bad service to develop a training tape which can be used to train new employees.

For in-person service, the same two methods apply, except the reviewer directly observes the employee and customer. Recordings can be audio or video. A helpful learning exercise is to ask the employee to complete the checklist after the audit and compare their scores with the reviewer's. It is often the case that an employee is unaware of stylistic deficiencies.

My first experience with recording service calls was revealing. We recorded the service calls of twelve bank telephone customer service representatives. They answered calls from phones located next to the bank's ATM's. I then met with bank operations management to play back some of the tapes. Regretably, I had not reviewed the tapes in advance. The first call came from a customer who was late for his plane and couldn't get the ATM to accept his card. After his complaint there was a long silence followed by "Wipe it on your butt!"

The startled customer asked the representative to repeat what she had said, and she did. The fourth call was from another harried customer who was standing in the rain. "Your stupid machine isn't working again!" The calm and pleasant response was, "I'm sorry sir. We have another ATM at our branch at the intersection of Vine and Cherry. It's only about ten blocks from your present location." The representative went on to provide the customer with detailed directions on how to get to the other branch. The management group was very satisfied with the call, until one of the managers stated that the branch the customer had been referred to had been closed over a year ago!

A review of the service training and tools, revealed that the representatives weren't trained, weren't provided a script, and had no reference material with which to solve customer problems. A service call model was designed and training conducted. The frequency of unsatisfactory service calls almost immediately fell to zero.

Customer Service Surveys.

Customer service surveys are essential to the effective operation of most organizations. As mentioned, even if service levels are monitored well, in most cases customer impressions are really more important than the actual service levels. An effective customer survey should consist of actionable items that can be related to specific employees or departments. It should survey a valid sample of customers, and it should be administered frequently.

1) **Actionable items.** Survey items should refer to specific, measurable and correctable employee actions. For example, the survey item "ACME provides superior service" is too vague. To correct a low score the employee would have to define the the terms 'superior' and 'service'. More actionable items would be "ACME's deliveries are on time," "When I call ACME, I am promptly referred to someone who can help me," "The ACME service representatives are cordial and helpful."

2) **Related to specific employees.** Where practical, the survey item should refer to a specific employee or department. General items do not pinpoint for whom an improvement plan needs to be implemented. The item should refer to a specific service, product line, location, or department whenever possible. On the other hand, it would be inconvenient for the customer if each department conducted its own survey. A solution is to create one survey with items that are coded to specific departments. The department would then receive results only on the items pertinent to them.

It is possible to obtain survey information on individual employees. This feedback will, of course, generate the most service improvement in the shortest period of time. One method we have used, is for the employee to hand the customer a survey card to complete after the transaction. The card has a unique employee identification number, which is used to sort responses by employee. For telephone or mail service, the employee identification number can be stated over the phone, or a business card placed in the correspondence.

3) **Valid Samples.** Two key issues affect survey sample validity. The first is ensuring that an adequate number of customers respond to the survey. Second, the survey technique should ensure the sample is representative of the total customer base. A common problem with customer initiated surveys like mail-in's, is that a disproportionate number of disgruntled customers may respond. There are at least two practical solutions to this issue. One solution is to use employee-initiated survey calls. One or more employees is assigned to call a sample of customers who have had recent transactions with the organization. This method allows the employee to probe further into customer service concerns. A second method is to reward customers for responding to a survey, The survey becomes a 'lottery ticket' and a drawing is held each quarter.

The following are two examples of paying customers to help the organization monitor its service levels. The first case occurred in the 1970s, when banks were just introducing automated teller machines (ATM's) to the public. The response was poor—very few customers were willing to transact their business with the ATM's. Several solutions had been tried, including posting people next to the ATM's to help customers learn to operate them. The solution I proposed, was to turn the ATM's into 'slot machines' that would immediately reward people for trying the machine. The ATM's were programmed on a probability basis to pay out different amounts up to a daily maximum. A no-payout condition was set for customers who 'played' more than three times a day. Non-customers could play by picking up a one-time identification number in the branch.

The results were much better than we had hoped. There were consistent lines in front of the 14 ATM's during most of the day. Spot checks found people using the ATM's in the middle of the night to avoid the lines. The percentage of the bank's transactions processed by ATM's rose from 13% to 27% over a three-month period. An unexpected side effect was that 400 non-customers opened accounts with the bank after participating in the program. The program ran for six months. After the program ended, there was no reduction in ATM usage, since the inherent convenience maintained customer behavior. Each time the bank installed a new ATM, the program was implemented at the ATM for a three-month period.

The second example involved getting customers to use a touch-screen customer survey kiosk. The kiosk was placed in the lobby of a hotel. The statistics for the first few weeks were disappointing. Only 15% of the customers took the survey. We then decided to add a lottery feature to the survey. Once the survey was completed, the customer could 'pick a lucky number' and win a prize. A receipt printer in the kiosk printed out the prize receipt immediately after the customer selected a lucky number. The percentage of customers taking the survey rose to 85% in the first week of the prize program.

4) **Frequent survey administration.** Many organizations conduct annual customer surveys. The shortcoming is that no trend in service can be established, since it would take three years (three data points) to even begin to observe trends over time. Absolute survey scores are difficult to interpret. Previous survey data is needed to

interpret the survey results trend. Further, annual survey data is too delayed to be much help in evaluating service improvement plans the organization might implement.

To increase the frequency of survey data, three solutions are presented: sampling, employee-initiated surveys and automated survey technology. One practical sampling method is to survey only a portion of the total customer base during each survey period. For example, one-fourth of the customer base could be surveyed each quarter. Alternatively, employee-initiated surveys often provide more valid samples, and do not rely totally on customer preferences for the survey to occur. Small monthly samples would be the ideal here.

The survey process can be integrated with the normal work flow. For example, customer service representatives could present a short survey to customers at the end of the telephone call. Some often overlooked survey delivery groups are both inside and outside sales employees, drivers, service technicians and others.

New technology makes surveying much less labor-intensive than previously. Automated phone survey systems are available, that record survey responses through the phone key pad and can also record customer's comments. We provide an employee survey of management skills to one client on an international basis. Employees call in and can take the survey in English, Spanish, French, Portugese, or German. An alternative to the 800 number automated telephone survey, is to make the survey an option in the organization's PBX menu.

Touch screen technology has already been described. More recent developments include e-mail and internet survey systems. Given these new technologies, there is no good reason for an organization not to survey its customers on a consistent basis.

Regulatory Compliance Performance Measures.

Regulatory compliance refers to an organization and its employees' compliance with governmental, professional or organizational policies and requirements. Common governmental agencies include OSHA, DOT, EPS, FDA, EEOC, and others. Examples of certifications are ISO 9000 and various requirements in the healthcare industry. The measurement techniques are similar, except where prescribed by the regulatory body itself.

Using safety as an example, the OSHA measure is recordable accidents per 100,000 work hours. Agency audit scores, fines, workman's compensation expense, and non-compliance citations are all useful measures, many of which are tracked as part of the normal business operations. However, in the majority of cases, prevention should be stressed rather than remediation. Airline crashes is a legitimate outcome measure of pilot safety – but hardly a means for preventing accidents. Due to frequent long delays and/or infrequent (but critical) occurrences, we suggest that behavioral checklist measures be implemented along with the more conventional outcome measures.

Since accidents, fines, or other penalties will likely affect the employee, the primary purpose of behavioral compliance measures is to remind or prompt compliant behaviors rather than reinforce them. For this unique reason, self-reported behavioral checklist data may prove more effective than an outcome measure. Alternatively, a check-list audit can be conducted by the manager or the quality manager.

Chapter 12

Performance Measurement: Project and Support Jobs

Project Measures.

Project performance refers to long-duration, one-time outcomes that involve several steps to complete. Project performance measurement categories include accuracy, timeliness, service, expense, and productivity.

Project Timeliness Measures.

Development Steps.

1. Select projects to be scored.

2. Divide the project into milestones that can be completed monthly, if possible.

  *Milestone is defined by a 'deliverable', a tangible result that provides evidence that the project has been completed up to that point.

  *Milestone is assigned a due date.

3. Assign the staff days allowed to complete a project.

  *Staff days are estimated by three independent estimators. Typically the estimators are the project manager, area manager, and the internal user.

  *Estimates are averaged to arrive at the allowed staff days.

4. Prorate the allowed staff days across the milestones as follows:

Three MS	Four MS	Five MS
1 20%	1 10%	1 10%
2 30%	2 20%	2 15%
3 50%	3 30%	3 20%
	4 40%	4 25%
		5 30%

Computing Monthly Project Scores

Each month, the year-to-date project days earned is compared to the year-to-date staff days due. For example:

Month	YTD Staff Days Due	YTD Staff Days Earned	Earned/Due
Jan	10	8	80%
Feb	25	25	100%
Mar	40	45	113%

In the above plan, credit is earned whenever the milestone is met. For most project tracking this is adequate.

(Optional) Adjusting Earned Days by Milestone Timeliness.

For each project, the date the project is officially assigned is recorded. Subsequent completion and due dates are referenced to this assigned date to compute a project timeliness percentage. The formula is:

(Due Date - Assigned Date) / (Completion Date - Assigned Date)

For example, a project is assigned January 5th. The first milestone is due January 20th. The staff days allocated to the milestone are 5.

The milestone is actually completed on January 25th. Therefore:

(20 - 5) / (25 - 5) = 75% x 5 staff days = 3.75 earned days. The performance score is 3.75 / 5 = 75% (first month of the year)

Project Scoring Form

Project Title_____

Assigned Date_____   Team Leader_____

Milestone	Assigned Date (A)	Milestone Due Date (B)	Completion Date (C)	Allocated Staff Days (D)	% On-time (B-A)/(C-A) (E)	Earned Days (D x E)
1						
2						
3						
4						
5						

Weighted percentage milestones meeting deadlines. To encourage programmers to meet deadlines early, and to complete projects past their deadline, this measure is an alternative to the "percent deadlines met" measure. To compute the measure, determine the number of days between the project or milestone, start date, and deadline (allowed days). When the project is completed, divide the number of days allowed by the actual number of days taken to complete the project. For example, a project is assigned 20 allowed days and is completed in 25 days. The performance percentage would be 20 / 25 or 80%.

For programmers working on multiple projects, you may also wish to weight each project's priority. You can cap each project at 100% of the weight, or you may want to encourage early completion by allowing the performance percentage to exceed 100%. Below is an example of the uncapped version of this approach.

Project	Start	Due	Allow	Actual	Perf %	Wgt	Wgt%
A	4/10	4/15	5	7	71%	30%	21.3
B	4/15	5/30	45	40	113%	70%	79.1
				Total Weighted Perf. =			100.4

Percent project priority weightings completed. A third approach is to assign a priority point value to each project. The programmer earns the points when a project is completed. The earned points are divided by the milestone points due in the month to compute the performance percentage. For example:

Project	Due	Earned
A	10	
B	20	20
C	15	
Totals	45	20

Performance % = 20/45 = 44%

Programming Measures

Accuracy Measures.

Percentage of maintenance updates passing Quality Audit

Percentage of updates operating for 'X' days without additional revision

Percentage of development projects not returned by user in 'X' days

Service Measures.

Customer Service Rating. An internal or external customer rating form can be developed, in which customers rate a programmer on several dimensions including accuracy, timeliness, service quality, etc. I recommend the form used be checklist style (yes/no), and relate to specific, objective outcomes rather than customer subjective impressions.

QC Service Rating. The user request document can be designed so that each request specification can be checked by a quality control employee, or the manager, upon completion of the project. This rating can augment, or replace, the customer rating.

Application Error Rate. The number of help calls, complaints, or application failures can be tracked for a specified post-installation period. A quality ratio can be used to adjust each application's error rating for application complexity, or number of end users. This weighting is then compared to the number of help calls, complaints, or failures.

Development Productivity Measures. Measuring the productivity of a development programmer is difficult. Lines of code produced per month is a flawed measure, since lines vary in complexity, and the programmer can increase lines of code by writing an inefficient program. For very precise measurements of development productivity, the reader is referred to "function point" analysis, standard time and other approaches outside the scope of this book.

One practical alternative, is to determine the key variables which affect programmer productivity, such as user input, tools, language, number of data files, number of screens, and so on. A scoring system can be designed for each variable. Each project is then scored on the various variables, and after several projects have been scored, a multiple regression equation is developed that weights the importance of each variable in terms of programmer hours required to complete the project.

Once the regression model is developed, future projects can be scored on the relevant variables to predict the required programmer hours and assign an incentive value to the project. Two commercial examples of this approach are 'Estimax' and 'Estimin.' A less technical approach is to have independent expert raters review several projects and then estimate the programmer hours it would take to complete the project. These estimates can be compared to the scores on several variables to develop a project scoring system.

Maintenance Productivity Measures. Maintenance productivity is simpler to measure than development. Assign a standard time value to each type of maintenance activity based on expert estimates, or an actual analysis. Each month multiply the number of maintenance projects completed by their standard times to compute "earned time." Divide earned time by actual hours to compute a productivity percentage (see data entry for a full description).

Expense Measures. An individual programmer, project team, or the programming department's expenses, can be compared to the number of projects completed, standard hours, or estimated revenue to compute an expense ratio. Typical expenses included in the expense ratio are prorated software and equipment purchases, computer time, and error expense for code that fails to perform.

Support Position Measures

Support positions, such as secretaries, administrative assistants, and other staff positions are difficult to measure, since the final results they produce are other employees' performance. This support role makes it difficult to develop on-going measures, or to audit measures, since the activities are sub-steps in a process rather than results. Some support positions include other job duties such as those of a customer service representative, word processor operator, data entry operator, or bookkeeper. In these instances, there are specific job measures described for these jobs. For support functions four approaches are used – linked performance measures, administrative checklists, special projects, and user surveys.

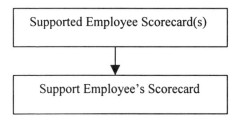

Support linked performance measures. The support employee is measured on the performance of the employee or employees they support. For example, a departmental secretary is measured on the average performance of the employees in the department. The departmental secretary's total score may be this average, or the average may be one measure on a scorecard that contains other measures of the secretary's performance.

Administrative Checklist. The support employee's direct supervisor develops a checklist of results to be accomplished during the month. These checklist items are stated as "yes/no" items, that is, done or not done. The checklist items should be objectively stated as a noun and past tense verb within a time frame. For example, 'report submitted by the 15th.' 'All documents assigned during the month typed without return within two days.' 'All documents filed by end of day.' Each item can be priority weighted. For example:

Sample Administrative Assistant Checklist

Task	Due by:	Days Credit	Earned Credit
Set up meeting	10/20	0.5	0.5
Organize files		2	2
Mail out agenda	10/10	0.5	0.5
Prepare new report		1	0
Prepare summary	10/31	1	1
Totals		5	4

Month's Score = 4 / 5 = 80%

Support Special Project Measures. Sometimes, support people are assigned substantial projects, or asked to work outside their assigned position for a long duration. These projects are outside assignments could simply be added to the checklist and provided a high 'days credit value.' However, if the checklist is one of several measures, the scorecard priority weightings would not equitably reflect the new project or assignment.

One simple approach to handle these situations, is to add a 'special projects' measure to the scorecard with a priority weighting added <u>above</u> the scorecard's 100%. When no special projects are assigned, the measure will have no effect on the scorecard score, due to the zero rating.

A base of 0% and a goal of 100% are assigned to the special project measure. When a special project is assigned, a percentage completed is entered as the monthly performance data, which is then multiplied by the priority weighting and added to the employee's overall score. One method for deciding the value of a special project, or outside assignment, is to divide the number of days assigned to the project, by the number of workdays in the month, and enter this percentage. Alternatively, the value of the project, relative to the other scorecard performances, can be judged and used to assign the percentage.

User survey measures. The support person, or team, can be rated by their internal users. We have had mixed results with this approach. It is often difficult to get other employees to rate co-workers accurately. This problem can be overcome, to some degree, by having the user rate each service event, rather than providing a general rating of the support person or team. A rating box is attached to each service document or the support group sends a rating form to each service user in the month. As with other surveys, the items should be behaviorally anchored, and the survey should consist of as few items as possible.

Bookkeeping

Bookkeeping performance measure categories include accuracy, timeliness, and sometimes productivity.

Accuracy and Timeliness Measures.

% Days out of balance. The number of days balanced compared to the number of days in the month. A simple measure to track that emphasizes the frequency of out-of-balance conditions over the amount of the error.

Average absolute dollars out of balance. The month's absolute total of overages and shortages for the month. This measure emphasizes error amount over error frequency.

% absolute dollars out of balance. Similar to average dollars out of balance, except the measure adjusts for the number and amounts of financial transactions in the month.

% days balanced by 3:00 P.M. The percentage of days in the month, the books are balanced by a predetermined time of day.

% reports on schedule. The percentage of required reports delivered on schedule.

For smaller companies whose bookkeepers perform several tasks, see also Purchasing, Collections, Credit, and Accounting plans.

Productivity Measures.

Bookkeeping labor expense/revenue. A general productivity measure that roughly relates to accounting productivity.

Transactions per labor hour. The number of transactions posted per month, divided by the number of bookkeeper labor hours.

Personnel Recruiters

Recruiters are personnel employees who recruit new hires for the organization. Recruiter performance categories can include accuracy, timeliness, expense and productivity.

Accuracy Measures.

Number of line manager applicant interviews per hire. A measure of the quality of applicants scheduled by the recruiter.

Percentage of applicants passing probation period. A measure of the quality of applicants submitted by the recruiter.

Average applicant first year performance appraisal, or performance index score. The average first quarter, or first year, appraisal ratings, or the performance index scores of all applicants hired by a recruiter.

Internal customer service rating. The average rating of the recruiter by the managers of all hiring departments.

% Regulatory Compliance. The percentage of applicants and interviews with proper regulatory documentation on file. (Audit conducted by recruiter's supervisor.)

% New Hire Attrition. The percentage of new hires who leave the organization within one (or two) years of hire date.

Timeliness Measures.

Average days to fill a request. The average number of days between a line request for an applicant interview, and the interview.

Percent requests meeting turnaround goal. The number of applicant interviews scheduled successfully within the turnaround goal time.

Average days to fill a position. The average number of days between a request for an employee, and an employee hire.

Expense Measures.

Payroll + Advertising + Phone + Agency Fees / # Interviews or # Hires

Any combination of relevant expenses may be applied as an expense measure

Productivity Measures.

Number of interviews / recruiter labor hours. The number of job interviews successfully scheduled, divided by the number of recruiter labor hours. If you want to encourage the recruiter to cross-train, modify the measure to "number of interviews / recruiter labor hours minus hours in other positions."

Combination Plans. You may combine specific job measures, linked scores, user ratings, and checklist scores in a performance matrix.

Training

Two types of trainer performance measures are described - full-time trainers, or training performed by managers and supervisors as part of their total job accountabilities. Full-time trainer performance dimensions may include accuracy, timeliness, service, and expense.

Accuracy Measures.

Pre-Post Test Improvement. The trainees' knowledge and/or skills can be assessed before, after training, and the percent improvement computed. These assessments can be written tests or job simulations. A job simulation is simply having the employee perform the job under controlled conditions, and scoring performance before training (i.e. a typing test). The same test, or an equivalent, is then given again after training. The post-test score minus the pre-test score divided by the pre-test score, computes the percentage improvement. For example, a data entry operator performs a simulation and operates at 1000 net items per hour. In the post-test he operates at 1600 net items an hour. The improvement percentage is (1600 - 1000) / 1000 = 600 / 1000 = 60% improvement.

Job Performance Improvement. If your organization has performance measures in place, the three-month average performance of the trainee before and after training, can be measured. For example, a supervisor sends an employee to training. The employee's three-month average performance before training is 40%. After training, the three-month average performance is 70%. The pre-post improvement is (60% - 40%) / 40% = 20% / 40% = 50%.

Trainee Performance. The days after training required to meet the job standard can be compared to goal as an alternative to the above accuracy measures. For example, the goal may be to have all trainees meet the performance standard within 30 days of training. The actual days are 40, so the percentage is 30 / 40 = 75%.

Learning Curve Progress. For jobs in which performance improves gradually over time, a learning curve can be developed from historical data. Trainee performance is then compared to the curve each month. For example:

Month	Standard	Actual Perf.
1	20%	30%
2	25%	30%
3	30%	30%
4	40%	30%
5	60%	50%
6	100%	90%

Timeliness Measures.

Training Delivery Response Time. The days between a line request for the training of an employee, and the start or completion of the training. For example, the goal may be that all training is provided within 60 days of a line request. When all requests are averaged we find an average response time of 40 days. The trainer's performance would be 60 / 40 = 150%.

Service Measure. Users can include line supervisors and managers as well as trainees. The users can rate the timeliness of training, the quality of training, and the results of training.

Expense Measure. Expenses can be compared to the number of trainees, classes, or instructional modules delivered in a month. Expenses may include training payroll, materials, and equipment rental expense. Training development expense may be prorated into current training expense over a two-year period. For example, the training payroll and other expenses to develop a training program totaled $18,000. The monthly prorated expense would be $18,000 / 24 months or $750 a month. This expense would be added to the current month's actual expenses to compute the training expense ratio.

Payroll and Benefits Manager/Staff

The Payroll and Benefits function's performance dimensions may include accuracy, timeliness, service, and expense.

Accuracy Measures.

Percent payroll checks correct. The number of checks distributed, minus the number of checks corrected, divided by the number of checks distributed.

Percent benefits statements correct. The number of statements distributed, minus the number requiring correction, divided by the number of statements distributed.

Percent claims funded. The number of claims submitted, minus claims not paid, divided by the number of claims submitted.

Timeliness Measures.

Percent checks on time. The number of checks distributed, minus the number of checks distributed late, divided by the number of checks distributed.

Percent benefits payments on time. The number of benefits claims submitted, minus the number paid late, divided by the number submitted.

Percent inquiry responses meeting response time goal. The number of employee inquiries, minus those not responded to within the goal response time, divided by the number of employee inquiries.

Service Measure.

User ratings of payroll/benefits performance can be obtained from employees, managers, and supervisors, as well as benefits vendors.

Expense Measures.

Payroll expense per employee. Typical expenses include computer time and outside vendor expenses.

Benefits expense per employee or as a percentage of payroll. A measure of the performance of the benefits employee in obtaining and maintaining low cost benefits programs.

SECTION III: PERFORMANCE PAY

Chapter 13

Alternative Pay Systems

In recent years. the use of incentive pay programs has increased dramatically. Not only are more companies implementing incentive pay programs, but they are implementing them for all employees, rather than the traditional senior management and sales programs. Furthermore, the diversity of plans is increasing with less reliance on conventional profit sharing and more on goal sharing, gainsharing and other innovative incentive strategies.

A company considering incentive pay, is faced with a rather bewildering array of alternatives. How does an organization determine which approach is best for them? This decision should be based upon the organization's objectives for the incentive program. Though there are many unique reasons an organization may consider in implementing an incentive pay program, five objectives stand out as universal issues.

Incentive Pay Objectives

1) Alignment. Today's rapidly changing business environment requires a 'nimble' organization. An organization that can respond quickly to new developments by changing direction and quickly bringing new products and services to market. One objective of an incentive pay plan, is to communicate new strategies and reward employees who assist in executing these strategies.

2) Focus. As jobs become more complex and dynamic, it is increasingly difficult to ensure employees focus on the key results and tactics which drive the organization's strategy and profits. Once a strategy is communicated, an incentive plan can assist in focusing employees on the key results that help execute the strategy.

3) **Performance.** Today's competitive business environment demands more from employees than ever before. As organizations become 'leaner', each employee's personal effectiveness becomes more critical. In addition, more demanding customers require higher levels of employee responsiveness and quality. An incentive program can assist in optmizing employee productivity and performance quality.

4) **Commitment.** Many organizations are concerned about key employee attrition. Generation 'X' employees are notorious for their commitment to their personal goals, rather than to their organization. The day when an individual joined an organization, and remained with it until retirement, seems to have passed. However, the organization still desires an employee group that provides continuity for its internal operations and customers, and delivers consistent, high quality performance. One objective of an incentive plan, then, is to increase employee commitment to the organization.

5) **Affordability.** Diminishing profit margins and uncertain futures are forcing organizations to better control their compensation expense. Incentive pay programs can index employee compensation to profitability, in order to effectively convert a portion of compensation from a fixed to a variable expense.

Incentive Pay Alternatives

Although there are many incentive pay schemes, four of the most common are commissions and piece rates, goal sharing, gainsharing and profit sharing. A fifth approach, which we term profit-indexed performance pay (PIPP), integrates key features of the other approaches.

Commissions and Piece-Rates. These programs are considered together, because they both pay per unit (revenue or piece). Pay-per-unit has a long history, but today is especially common for sales people. Pay-per-unit plans often include a threshold performance level above which payments are made. Below threshold, the employee receives only base pay or a draw. Many plans, especially commission plans, increase the pay-per-unit as predefined performance levels or 'hurdles' are met.

Goal Sharing. Goal sharing is fairly common for senior managers, and is increasingly being applied to other employees. Typically, annual goals are established for key performances such as profits, sales, projects, meeting budget, and many others. These plans vary widely in terms of their specifics. Some pay, only if the goal is achieved, while others pay for a percentage of achievement.

The amount of the payment may differ among the objectives. In some cases, payments are conditional and adjusted for profitability, or other personal or organizational factors. In most cases, the payment is 'capped' and cannot exceed a predefined amount or percentage of salary. These plans are usually applied to individuals, but team plans are becoming more common.

Gainsharing. Gainsharing plans were first introduced around fifty years ago–primarily in manufacturing. They are typically driven by annual productivity improvements over the previous year. Gainshare plans are group plans in which management, or all employees, are awarded a share of the savings. The distribution is often based upon each employee's wage or salary, as a percentage of the total payroll.

Profit Sharing. In this context, profit sharing refers to annual cash awards to employees based upon predefined profit levels. Profit sharing that funds retirement is here considered a benefit plan rather than an incentive plan. The concept of profit sharing is quite old, dating back to farming in feudal times and more recently 'share cropping'. As with gainshare plans, profit sharing is a group plan in which management, or all employees, are awarded a share of the profits over a predefined threshold. The share is sometimes based upon each employee's wage or salary as a percentage of the total payroll.

Profit-Indexed Performance Pay (PIPP). PIPP integrates goal sharing and profit sharing. Incentive pay opportunity is determined by the organization's (or some sub-group's) profitability. Unlike profit sharing, however, the distribution is adjusted for personal or team performance on predefined measures and goals. Abernathy & Associates has assisted many organizations in designing and implementing this type of plan.

Comparison of the Different Plans' Effectiveness

Plan Type	Align	Focus	Perform	Commit	Afford
Commission/Piece-Rate		✓	✓		
Goal Sharing	✓	✓	✓		
Gain Sharing			✓		✓
Profit Sharing				✓	✓
Profit-Indexed Performance Pay	✓	✓	✓	✓	✓

Commission and Piece-rate plans focus employees on one performance dimension – sales or production. Because incentive payments are not adjusted for profitability or other factors, the plan is exceptionally reliable in its payouts. This typically leads to higher performance levels than more complex plans.

These plans are not indexed to profitability, and therefore can generate substantial payouts in unprofitable periods. The narrow focus of the plans on sales and production, can lead to unbalanced performance in which quality and teamwork suffer. Furthermore, the plans are not aligned with the organization's long-term strategic goals. Commissions and piece rates are known for creating 'Lone Rangers' who have no personal investment in the organization, and will move elsewhere if a better opportunity arises.

Goal Sharing plans establish specific measures and goals for individuals or teams which provide a high degree of focus (assuming the number of measures is reasonable). These specific measures typically produce high performance levels, though less so than one-dimensional commissions and piece rates. If the measures are designed to drive strategic objectives, these plans can improve the alignment of employee goals with the organization's strategy.

Goal sharing plans are typically 'capped' at a percentage of the employee's salary. As a consequence, the plan 'caps out' at some predetermined percentage of the employee's salary regardless of the success of the organization. This feature disconnects the employee from ownership, whose earnings are only limited by the organization's ability to generate additional profits. As a result, the employee's long-term commitment to the organization is compromised. Further, because goal share plans are not indexed to organizational profitability, they can pay out in unprofitable periods. Some organizations conduct post hoc analyses of the return on incentive investment from these plans. These analyses are quite imprecise for performance measures other than sales and productivity.

Gainsharing research has found that these plans do improve productivity. They provide a predetermined return on incentive investment to the organization since they are after-the-fact shares of actual savings. Similar to commissions and piece rate plans, gainshare plans do not include quality or strategic issues, and therefore are not aligned with the organization's long-term objectives. Because gainshare plans are group plans, they fail to focus employees on specific performances or recognize personal contributions. This fact, combined with gainshare's requirement for ever-increasing productivity, make these plans poor candidates for securing employee commitment.

Profit Share plans can create employee 'stakeholders', who are committed to the organization's long-term success, because the organization is willing to share this success with them (similar, in concept, to partners in a professional corporation). Profit sharing is the most 'affordable' plan of the four described since it only awards payments if a true profit above threshold occurs.

However, profit sharing fails to specify each employee's role in the company's strategy. In addition to this lack of alignment, the group nature of the plan does not provide any employee focus or feedback, and therefore does little to foster performance improvement. Finally, profit sharing pays all employees similarly, regardless of their personal contributions.

Profit-Indexed Performance Pay (PIPP) integrates goal sharing and profit sharing, to provide the benefits of both. Correctly implemented, this plan meets all five previously listed objectives. However, PIPP is more complex than commission or piece rate plans, and will therefore likely not produce the short-term level of sales or productivity improvements, offered by commissions and piece rates. Furthermore, its complexity requires effective and continuous communications to ensure the plan's success.

Chapter 14

Phase I: Profit-Indexed Performance Pay

Profit-Indexed Performance Pay

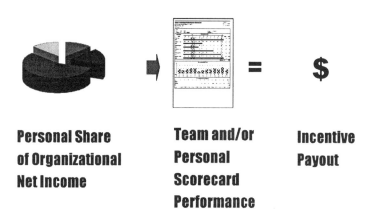

Personal Share of Organizational Net Income → **Team and/or Personal Scorecard Performance** = **Incentive Payout**

The conventional wage and salary system became the dominant way to pay people in the years following World War II. It was spawned in an era of high inflation, high consumer demand, and full employment. Today, this approach to pay is a millstone around the necks of most organizations. It is a system that: 1) fosters a low-performance, entitlement mentality; 2) relies on management by exception (negative reinforcement) to motivate workers; 3) disconnects employees from their organization's business strategy; and 4) forces companies to underpay employees in growth years, and to downsize in declining years.

An alternative to the conventional wage and salary system, is to consider employees to be partners or stakeholders in the business. Wages and salaries are gradually, partially replaced by monthly profit sharing to a below-market target level. Employee profit sharing is adjusted by personal and/or team scorecard performance. An employee's personal performance or his team's performance, determines his share. The four elements of Profit-Indexed Performance Pay (PIPP) are: the base pay (wage or salary); the employee opportunity basis; the organizational opportunity multiplier; and the performance scorecard score. These four elements are multiplied to compute the employee's performance pay.

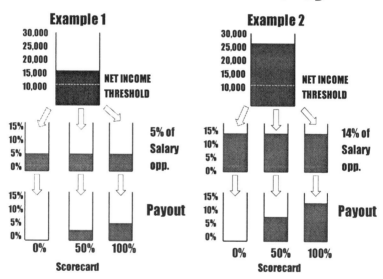

Base Pay. The employee's base pay is set comparable to local wage and salary market practices. The 'mid-point' of the wage, or salary scale, is set at the average market price of the job. A pay band around this mid-point describes the highest and lowest pay associated with the job. Where an employee falls within this pay band is based on his education, experience, and tenure. The incentive pay opportunity is indexed to the employee's job position mid-point in the pay range, or to the employee's actual pay. This indexing ensures the incentive opportunity reflects the 'commodity' or 'market' value of the job.

PIPP Basis. Each employee is assigned a personal PIPP *basis* which determines her incentive pay opportunity. The basis is defined as a percentage of the employee's wage or salary. It is assigned for one year and reviewed annually. The basis percentage can vary among employees. Rationales for assigning different bases include the employee's level in the organization, incentive pay substitution for the annual salary increase, below-market base pay, acquisition of new skills, and to recruit and retain employees in key positions.

When PIPP replaces existing bonus or incentive plans, the basis should ensure an equal or better than incentive opportunity in comparison to the previous plan. Organizations that are implementing PIPP, and are not replacing previous plans, often begin with an across-the-board five-percent basis for workers and a ten-percent basis for managers. This differential is justified, in that the major change effort required to implement PIPP is made by management, more so than workers.

PIPP Multiplier. The basis incentive opportunity is adjusted by a profit multiplier each month or quarter. The multiplier typically ranges from 0.0 to 3.0. If an employee's basis was 5%, the multiplier would adjust the basis over a range from 0% (5% x 0) to 15% (5% x 3.0) for workers, and 0% (10% x 0) to 30% (10% x 3) for managers. If the organization desires a minimum opportunity each payout period, the multiplier can be set to range from 1.0 to 3.0, which would ensure a minimum 5% opportunity for workers and 10% for managers.

Multiplier Range. The multiplier range can be expanded annually to compensate for increases in scorecard goal requirements. For example, if the scorecard goals were increased an average 20%, the multiplier could be increased 20% from 3.0 to 3.6. This practice allows the organization to adopt a continuous improvement philosophy without reducing employee incentive pay opportunity. In highly leveraged systems, the organization should consider 'uncapping' the multiplier range, since employees have truly 'invested' in the company.

Threshold. Minimum return to ownership, debt service, reserves, capital expenditures, and expenses over which employees have no control should make up the 'threshold' or zero point on the multiplier scale. This prevents wide swings in incentive opportunity that are unrelated to employee performance. Since expenses budgeted in the threshold are covered before profit sharing occurs, they therefore do not need to be included in the profit multiplier controllable net income.

Controllable Net Income Computation Level There are basically three methods used in PIPP for establishing the employee incentive opportunity. The opportunity can be determined by the overall organizational profitability; sub-sets of the organization such as regions, business lines, or profit centers; or the opportunity can be disconnected from profitability and simply budgeted. The illustration on the following page depicts these alternatives.

Determining Incentive Pay Opportunity

Conservative ⇒ Aggressive

Incentive pay opportunity based on:

Company Net Income → **Department/ Branch Net Income** → **Budgeted Incentives**

1. **Budgeted Incentive Opportunity.** This approach to incentive funding is the simplest and most motivational for employees. A fixed percentage of salary becomes the incentive opportunity and is budgeted for each employee. How much of the budgeted opportunity is earned, is determined by multiplying the scorecard percentage by the budgeted incentive opportunity percentage. The employee knows in advance, for the entire year, how much incentive opportunity there is.

There are two drawbacks to this approach to funding incentive pay. First, it is possible for the organization to make little profit and be faced with a substantial incentive pay expenditure. Disconnecting incentive pay from profitability is therefore a risky proposition for an organization. A significant percentage of scorecard measures address strategic or quality issues. Employees could achieve one-hundred percent of their goals without any effect on short-term profitability. Further, sharing profit recognizes unmeasured work that improves profits, and therefore incentive pay opportunity. Budgeted incentives do not reward unmeasured work.

The second drawback is that budgeted incentives do not provide a failsafe against implementing scorecard measures which have no impact on the organization's profitability. Budgeted incentives will pay out, even if the measures paid on have no effect on short or long-term profits. Over time, the measurement system could drift toward activity measures. In a profit-indexed system, activity measures could also be designed to always guarantee employees one hundred percent of goal. However, because the incentive opportunity is determined by profitability, employees would receive one-hundred percent of a zero incentive opportunity.

A compromise is to scale the multiplier from 1 to 3 rather than 0 to 3. This scale guarantees employees a minimum opportunity equal to their assigned basis percentage. In effect, the basis opportunity is budgeted with additional opportunity as profitability allows.

2. Departmental, Location, or Profit Center Determined Incentive Opportunity. This approach to funding incentives determines incentive pay opportunity based upon profitability computed below the level of the total organization. The level could be a division, business line, region, location or profit center. It is also possible to fund operational areas that do not produce revenue by employing an expense-to-volume ratio rather than net income. Savings produced by lowering the ratio fund the incentive opportunity.

The fewer employees assigned to the funding index, the better the employee 'line-of-site'. Employees are more empowered to affect the result. However, as funding moves further away from the net income of the total organization, the risk of payouts when total profits are low is increased. That is, some profit centers could generate payouts, while poor performance in others results in overall low profitability. One compromise is to create two funding sources. Two multiplier scales are implemented – one based on organizational net income and the other on profit center net income. The opportunities can then be summed to compute the total opportunity. Alternatively, a more conservative approach would be to fund the first half of the multiplier scale based on organizational net income, with the latter half-based on profit center net income.

3. **Total Organization Determined Incentive Opportunity.** Incentive opportunity is usually determined by the total organization's net income. This is the most conservative approach, since no opportunity is presented unless the organization's overall performance warrants it. This approach is recommended for small-to-medium sized organizations. In larger organizations, this type of funding may be too removed from the line employee, and may fail to generate employee buy-in or improvement efforts. To improve this situation, an 'open-book management' strategy can be employed, which provides financial information and projections to employees in large organizations.

Performance Score. The employee's incentive opportunity is multiplied by his scorecard index to compute the actual payout. The incentive payout formula options are:

Budgeted: Incentive Payout = Salary x Basis % x Performance Score

Profit-Indexed: Incentive Payout = Salary x Basis % x Profit Multiplier x Performance Score

If the organization never intends to assign different basis percentages to employees, the formula can be simplified by replacing the multiplier scale with a scale that directly converts net income to a percentage of base pay opportunity. For example:

Net Income	% Base Pay Incentive Opportunity
$100,000	0 %
$150,000	1 %
$200,000	2 %

In this case, the incentive payout formula is:

Incentive Payout = Salary x % Opportunity x Performance Score

Payout Frequency. Scorecards should be computed and distributed at least monthly, to provide sufficient performance feedback to identify performance trends and to evaluate improvement efforts. If monthly payouts are awarded, it is recommended that the payout be computed on a three-month, moving average of the net income. The payout amount should also be reported monthly, although the actual payout can occur quarterly or possibly less often.

Organizational Multiplier Scale Design Steps.

STEP 1. Define Controllable Net Income Elements.

The actual pre-tax, net income of the organization is used to fund the incentive pay opportunity if the revenues and expenses are generally influenced by employees. If there are revenues or expenses that are not influenced by employees, but have a significant impact on the net income, these elements are termed 'uncontrollable', and should be budgeted as part of the profit multiplier threshold. Examples of uncontrollable expenses are the cost of raw materials, interest expense, leases, and depreciation.

Another way to determine which revenues and expenses to include in the net controllable income is to consider which revenues and expenses the organization wants employees to focus on and have a voice in determining. For example, if marketing expense is included, then employees will attempt to reduce this expense and will expect to have some say in the marketing budget. This may be undesirable for the organization, because employees may take the 'short view', rather than the 'long view', in helping to control marketing expense. Similar issues arise with new technology and expansions. Classifying these expenses as uncontrollable, and budgeting them in the multiplier threshold, avoids these issues.

STEP 2. Define the Multiplier Scale Threshold.

In addition to budgeted uncontrollable expenses, a minimum return on investment for ownership, a reserve, and debt pay-down may be added to the threshold. Those expenses are summed to compute the multiplier scale threshold. The threshold represents the zero point on the multiplier scale. No employee incentive opportunity is made available until this point is surpassed. The threshold remains the same for one year, and is then adjusted annually to reflect changes in the threshold elements.

STEP 3. Define the Multiplier Scale Interval.

The multiplier scale is typically implemented with a range from 0.00 to 3.00. To design the scale, the net income required for a multiplier of 1.00 is computed. From this interval, all other intervals are interpolated. The following procedure is suggested for computing the multiplier intervals:

> a. Compute the total potential incentive payout expense when the multiplier interval is 1.00. This is accomplished by multiplying the payroll (excluding benefits, but including any current bonuses) by the employee incentive basis percentages. If different bases are assigned, multiply each group's total payroll by the assigned basis percentage. Sum all these calculations to compute the total incentive liability at a multiplier of 1.00.
>
> b. Define a 'share percentage'. The share percentage is the percentage of each net income dollar above threshold, that will be assigned as a potential incentive payout. The share percentage can be defined by management,

or can be computed by dividing the current total payroll by the current total revenue. The logic behind this computation, is that this percentage represents the percentage of each revenue dollar which is currently 'shared' with employees in the form of conventional compensation. For example, if the current monthly payroll is $200,000, and the average monthly revenue is $500,000, then the current 'share' is $200,000, divided by $500,000 or 40%.

c. Divide the total incentive potential by the share percentage to compute the multiplier scale interval. Add this to the threshold, to compute the net income required to generate a multiplier scale value of 1.00. For example, if the total incentive potential (step a) was $20,000 a month, we would divide $20,000 by (step b) 40% = $50,000 to compute the scale interval. When controllable net income is $50,000 above the scale threshold, employee incentive opportunity will equal the assigned opportunity basis.

d. Prorate this interval into sub-intervals to complete the scale. The author uses an eleven-point scale similar to the scorecard scale. These intervals are:

0.00
0.50
1.00
1.25
1.50
1.75
2.00
2.25
2.50
2.75
3.00

Any alternative number of intervals can be employed. Or, instead of an interval scale, a continuous scale may be implemented using the formula: (Actual net income minus Threshold) / ((Net Income at 1.00 minus Threshold)

Example:

STEP 1. The organization decides to exclude materials expense from the net income. This expense is budgeted at $100,000 a month for the year.

STEP 2. A minimum investor return of $50,000 a month is required. The two elements are summed to produce a threshold of $100,000 + $50,000 = $150,000.

STEP 3a. The organization decides to provide managers a 10% basis, and all other employees a 5% basis. The monthly payrolls of these two groups are multiplied by their bases, to compute the total potential incentive expense for a 1.00 multiplier.

Position	Total Payroll	Basis	Incentive Liability
Managers	$60,000	10%	$6,000
Employees	$160,000	5%	$8,000
Total			$14,000

STEP 3b. The current average monthly payroll is $220,000 while the average monthly revenue is $600,000. Dividing $220,000 / $600,000 yields a 36% current share, which is rounded to 35%.

STEP 3c. Dividing the total incentive potential by the share percentage yields $14,000 / 35% = $40,000. The multiplier interval is, then, $40,000.

STEP 4. The scale value of 0.00 is the threshold of $150,000. The scale value of 1.00 is the interval ($40,000) plus the threshold

($150,000) or $190,000. The remaining scale values are interpolated.

The complete eleven-point scale is:

Multiplier	Controllable Net Income	
0.0	$150,000	
0.50	$170,000	($150,000 + 0.50 x $40,000)
1.00	$190,000	($150,000 + 1.00 x $40,000)
1.25	$200,000	($150,000 + 1.25 x $40,000)
1.50	$210,000	($150,000 + 1.50 x $40,000)
1.75	$220,000	($150,000 + 1.75 x $40,000)
2.00	$230,000	($150,000 + 2.00 x $40,000)
2.25	$240,000	($150,000 + 2.25 x $40,000)
2.50	$250,000	($150,000 + 2.50 x $40,000)
2.75	$260,000	($150,000 + 2.75 x $40,000)
3.00	$270,000	($150,000 + 3.00 x $40,000)

STEP 5. The final scale is then validated by looking up the three month average controllable net income for each of the previous year's months. An average multiplier of 1.00 or better is optimal. If the payout is consistently zero, the design assumptions should be evaluated.

Prior Existing Bonus and Commission Conversion Procedures.

Organizations with existing bonus, profit sharing, gainsharing or sales commission plans should strongly consider consolidating them in the PIPP system. If such plans are allowed to continue parallel with PIPP, the strategic balance of the scorecards may be undermined, the plan will not guarantee a profit-indexed (variable) incentive expense return, and the system may be inequitable, since some employees would participate in two incentive programs.

To ensure the PIPP incentive opportunity is at least equivalent to previous incentive plans, the participants' previous year's (or an average of two or three years) total bonus is divided by the employee's annual base pay. This percentage becomes the new PIPP basis, or preferably, a basis greater than this is assigned. The greater basis accounts for the fact that PIPP payouts are adjusted for scorecard performance, while many bonus plans make no such adjustment.

Commission plans can be treated in the same way as bonus plans. However, if there is a desire to keep the commission performance requirements the same under PIPP, this can be accomplished by setting the salesperson's basis such, that meeting the goal when the multiplier value is at a 1.00, awards the same dollars as the original commission plan.

For example, a simple commission plan might award 5% of the revenue to the salesperson. If the monthly sales average $100,000, payouts would have been $5,000. If the salesperson's salary is $50,000, this payout represents $5,000 / $50,000 = 10% of the salary. Assigning a basis of 10% would pay the sales person the same as the original commission, when profitability is modest (multiplier = 1.00.) Higher profits would increase the commission, if the profits generated a PIPP multiplier above 1.00.

On the other hand, profits below a PIPP of 1.00, would mean the sales person would receive a payment less than the original commission, or no incentive payment at all below threshold. In this scenario, the salesperson risks the commission when the organization is unprofitable, but can triple the commission when the organization is successful. Alternatively, the salesperson's basis could be budgeted without applying the multiplier. This arrangement would duplicate the original commission arrangement.

Chapter 15

Phase II: Stakeholder Pay

Conventional Pay.

Wages and salaries are traditionally based on 'commodity' thinking. That is, an employee's value to the company is determined by the typical pay employees in the local area receive for the same job with the same experience and education. A salary survey is conducted to arrive at what the local market is paying. In contrast, performance pay is like the pay of a self-employed person. The self-employed person earns as much, or as little, as his business produces. There is no guarantee, but there is also no pay 'band' above which the employee cannot rise without additional experience, education or a promotion. The following diagram illustrates the differences between market-driven pay and performance pay.

I. Conventional Wage and Salary System

```
|
|                    Maximum of Pay Band
|············································
|
|_ _ _ _ _ _ _ _ _ _ _ _ _ _ _ _ _ _ _
|
|                    Local Market Average
|
|
|_____
```

II. Conventional Wage and Salary Plus Modest Performance Pay Opportunity

Incentive Pay Opportunity

Maximum of Pay Band

Local Market Average

III. Stakeholder Pay: Below-Market Base Pay with Well Above Market Performance Pay Opportunity

Performance Pay Opportunity

Local Market Average

Guaranteed Pay

In example I, the wage or salary 'mid-point' is indexed to local pay practices for similar jobs. A 'pay band' is applied around the mid-point. The employee's pay cannot exceed the upper limit of the pay band. To secure additional pay, the employee would have to change jobs, or receive a promotion.

In example II, an increasingly more common practice is to add an annual bonus to the base compensation. The bonus is not guaranteed, but does allow the employee to earn a modest percentage above market.

Example III describes 'stakeholder pay,' in which the guaranteed wage or salary is below market, but the performance pay opportunity is well above market. This approach to pay is the topic of this chapter.

Benefits of Stakeholder Pay.

Organizational Benefits. Indexing a portion of pay to organizational profitability converts that portion of the organization's fixed payroll expense to a variable expense. This conversion helps ensure a good profit margin, even during business declines. Indexed pay allows the organization to retain its workforce during down periods, thus avoiding costly layoffs. Furthermore, this enhanced job security improves employee loyalty and reduces turnover. The logic of stakeholder pay was outlined by the economist Martin Weitzman in his book *The Share Economy*.

The profit-indexed pay described in the previous chapter, adjusts payouts for personal and/or team scorecard performance. As a result, the distribution of profits is based on employee contribution and is more equitable than a simple, across-the-board inflation adjustment. Employees who consistently perform well, share in the profits more than those who do not. This practice recognizes high performer contributions and therefore increases the likelihood high performers will remain loyal to the organization and that average employees will strive to improve. Conventional pay is analogous to socialism, where profit-indexed performance pay's analog is the free market.

Benefits to Employees. By necessity, conventional guaranteed pay restricts the pay opportunities of employees. Even when the organization experiences high profits, these profits are rarely passed on to employees, because they become a future, fixed cost. This increased fixed cost creates problems for the organization when the eventual business downturn occurs. Profit-indexed pay places no such restriction on employee pay increases. Just as a self-employed person has no limit on earnings opportunity, the same is true for an employee in a profit-indexed pay organization. The only pay constraint is the creativity and competitiveness of the employee's organization.

Replacing 'commodity' pay with profit-indexed pay is especially beneficial to entry-level and unskilled workers. In the conventional pay system, the entry level worker must let time pass to see her pay increase to the upper limit of the pay band. The unskilled worker has little commodity value, and is doomed to low pay for his entire work life. Profit-indexed pay may be the only way out of this trap for these people, in the same way that immigrants have succeeded through entrepreneurship.

Although the employee takes a risk in a profit-indexed pay system, it is much less a risk than the hazards of self-employment. The infrastructure and customer base are already in place in an existing organization, while the failure rate of new businesses is some seventy percent over the first three years. The current pay system forces the entrepreneurial employee to quit the company and, often, to become a competitor. Profit-indexed pay makes a partner and stakeholder of the entrepreneurial employee, who can achieve his goals without leaving the organization.

As important as pay opportunity may be, job satisfaction is also a result of the work itself. Many theories of job satisfaction argue that supervision and job roles are more important than pay in creating job satisfaction. Examples of this view include job enlargement, job enrichment, self-directed teams, employee empowerment, open-book management and others. Although the issues are real, these programs do not seem to have a lasting impact on employee performance or commitment. I believe this is because the programs have the 'cart before the horse'. An employee who produces the minimum, and defers decision-making and accountability to others, does so for a reason. Similarly, an employee who expands her job role and increases personal decision-making and responsibility, also does so for a reason. In some situations I seek out new tasks and responsibility – in others I avoid them.

The first day of Army basic training, the sergeant asked our company if any of us had office skills. Thinking I could get out of the rigors of physical training and general hazing, I volunteered. The assignment proved to be picking up trash and cleaning restrooms after the day was over. I quickly learned not to volunteer again. And this is exactly what the Army wanted. They did not want self-directed, empowered soldiers–they wanted soldiers who would take orders without questioning.

As described in the earlier 'Sin of Wages' chapter, the wage and salary system also relies on intimidation (negative reinforcement) to manage workers. The relation between pay and performance is that pay continues as long as the employee performs to at least minimum expectations. This practice discourages proactivity and personal accountability. In profit-indexed performance pay, the employee can directly affect his pay. The better he and his organization perform, the greater the earnings. This contingent relationship between effort and reward encourages the development of new skills and personal decision-making and – ultimately – personal job satisfaction.

Employee Risk-Taking Factors.

An employee's willingness to share risks and rewards with the organization is determined by both personal and organizational risk factors. Employees will be unreceptive to becoming stakeholders in an organization if the perceived risks are too great. These risks are:

Personal Risk Factors

1. *Skills - Do I have the skills needed to consistently achieve the scorecard goals? If not, will the organization provide me the necessary training?*

Management and team member's willingness to coach, train, and assist employees address this concern.

2. *Effort - Will the scorecard goals be attainable, or will the risk and effort be too great?*

This issue is addressed by introducing the system in Phase I, without any downside pay-at-risk. If the employee succeeds in the Phase I system, she will be much more receptive to stakeholder pay. Success can be ensured through realistic goal-setting practices, and a consistent and meaningful incentive pay opportunity. Further, a true sense of empowerment is developed, if the manager and team work together to design and implement successful Tactical Improvement Plans.

3. *Investment - Do I have too much at stake in the current pay and recognition system? Will I fare as well in the new system?*

Employees who have invested a lot of time and effort in the current system will sometimes be the least receptive to the transition to stakeholder pay. Management is often surprised to discover that key employees, in the conventional system, are the most resistant to change. On reflection, however, the reasons are clear. An employee, who consistently receives high evaluations on the traditional subjective annual review, has more to lose in an objective measurement system than does the employee who is not in favor with his superiors. In fact, an employee who has come to be perceived as a poor performer, can only improve his situation if the organization moves to objective performance measures – there is little downside risk for these employees.

The organization can address the current top performer's concerns, by assuring them the measurements and incentive pay are not a total replacement for the subjective, annual performance review. The performance scorecard does not attempt to measure employee performance dimensions like attendance, punctuality, cooperation, responsiveness, honesty, creativity, and others. These dimensions usually require a more subjective interpretation but are, nevertheless, important considerations.

Organizational Risk Factors

1. *Faith - Will the company obtain consistent profits and continual growth? If not, the conversion to profit-indexed performance pay is a poor investment for the employee.*

The conversion to PIPP asks employees to invest a portion of their guaranteed pay, and pay increases, in the performance of the company. Faith in the company's ability to perform requires both open-book management and consistent marketing of the organization's strategy to its employees. The same practices that create and retain shareholders in the company, should be applied to employees in a stakeholder pay system.

2. *Trust - Will the organization consistently share profits with employees, or will they alter the share formula and requirements to reduce the share over time?*

A common mistake organizations make is too frequent changes to their bonus or incentive pay system opportunities and requirements. These practices reduce employee trust in the reliability of stakeholder pay as an alternative to conventional guaranteed pay. The first solution is to establish employee trust by limiting changes to an annual review, and to specify in writing the criteria that will be used to indicate a change is needed. Second, ownership and management must avoid the temptation to alter scorecard measures and goals, or the incentive multiplier scale, simply because some employees complain, there is a business downturn, or the inverse, the payouts are perceived as too great. The conventional salary system would not be viable, either, if the salary commitment changed in an unpredictable way.

3. *Opportunity - Can I influence my assigned scorecard measures and will the performance goals be attainable?*

To simplify design and administration, many organizations implement financial measures to determine incentive payouts for large groups of employees. To ask an employee to invest personal pay in these measures is more like gambling than entrepreneurship. Performance measures should be developed that can be directly influenced by small teams and individuals. Goals should be set to achieve the organizational strategy. Once this is accomplished, the goal should not be increased simply because employees are achieving it. Profit-indexed pay is not gainsharing. The fallacies in the gainsharing approach have already been described.

4. *Help - If I am not able to earn a good score on the scorecard, will my manager, co-workers, Human Resources, and others assist me?*

The Total Performance System is not intended to be a 'survival of the fittest' system that simply underpays, and eventually drives off, poor performers. This approach to performance improvement is expensive, and will not foster an entrepreneurial organizational culture, or encourage independent decision-making. The objective is to improve the performance of all employees.

Two Transition Strategies Toward Stakeholder Pay.

There are a number of potential obstacles to overcome when making the transition from guaranteed, market-comparable wages and salaries, to profit-indexed performance pay. The transition should usually not be attempted until a market guarantee, plus modest incentive opportunity system, has proven itself (Phase I). Two transition strategies are recommended.

Profit-Indexed Pay Increases. This transition strategy substitutes increased profit-sharing opportunity for annual wage and salary increases. This is accomplished by annually increasing each employee's 'basis' percentage. It is recommended that for every one percent of base pay increase that is given up, a one-percent increase in the incentive basis be awarded. For example, if the local market is providing employees an average four-percent base pay increase, the basis would also be increased four percent. Since the incentive multiplier scale typically ranges from zero to three, a 3 x 4% or 12% increase has, in effect, been awarded.

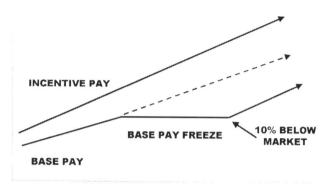

Reinstitute Base Pay Increases when Below Market Target is Met.

The organization establishes a 'below-market' base pay goal. For example, suppose an organization establishes a below-market base pay percentage in such a way that employees will ultimately be paid 90% of their market value. This would mean that an employee in a job with a market value of $20,000 a year would be paid $20,000 x .90 =$18,000. However, the above-market opportunity would be three times the risk, or 3 x 10% = 30%. Incentive earnings could be as much as $20,000 x 1.30 = $26,000, if the organization's profits warrant, and the employee achieves the scorecard goals throughout the year. To get to the below-market pay goal, a base pay freeze is instituted for as many years as it takes to achieve the pay leveraging goal. When the goal is achieved, the base pay increases are reinstituted. The illustration above describes this process.

An organization might elect to arrive at the below-market goal over a longer period and award half the market base pay increase each year rather than a total freeze. An organization with a goal of ten percent below market base pay would meet the goal in two to three years if the average market increase was four percent but would require four to six years to meet the goal with a partial freeze. The freeze should normally be applied only to employees who are at, or above, the salary mid-point, since this should represent average market pay.

Voluntary Stakeholder Plan. An alternative strategy for achieving stakeholder pay, is to provide employees the choice to participate in an immediate pay reduction. One approach, is to enable employee's to choose one of three levels of stakeholding. For example, a 5, 10, or 15% reduction in pay in exchange for a basis increase that would add a 15, 30, or 45% incentive opportunity. To manage this transition, and to ensure the transition's success, it is recommended that only top scorecard performers be eligible to participate. Furthermore, a ninety-day 'grace period' should be implemented. At the end of 90 days, the employee can choose to return to the original base pay and incentive opportunity. If this choice is made, the employee cannot again volunteer to become a stakeholder thereafter. The duration of the grace period would depend upon the consistency of incentive earnings opportunity for employees.

Transition to an Entrepreneurial Workplace

CUSTOMER MANAGED EMPLOYEES				PHASE II: VARIABLE PAY
POSITIVE LEADERSHIP			PHASE I: PROFIT-INDEX PERF. PAY	
DIRECT SUPERVISION	CONVENTIONAL WAGE & SALARY			
		GUARANTEED MARKET PAY + ANNUAL PAY INCREASES	GUARANTEED MARKET PAY + PROFIT-INDEXED PERF. PAY	BELOW MARKET PAY + HIGH PROFIT-INDEXED PERF. PAY

The table on the previous page illustrates the transition process. The typical organization begins with guaranteed market pay and annual market-based pay increases. Because the pay is guaranteed, the organization must rely on direct supervision and negative reinforcement to manage employees. In Phase I of the transition, a modest (5-15%) percentage of base pay incentive opportunity is awarded to employees, when profits permit and scorecard performance is achieved.

The addition of incentive pay and training in performance management and improvement, enables the manager to move away from the traditional direct supervision and intimidation role to a 'positive leadership' approach, in which the manager assists employees in meeting their scorecard goals. In Phase I, the base pay remains at market and annual increases are still awarded.

In Phase II, using either a base pay freeze, or voluntary pay reduction strategy (or both), the organization reduces the guaranteed base pay to some predefined below-market level, while increasing the incentive opportunity threefold. If the below market pay and above market incentive opportunity are significant, the need for traditional direct supervision diminishes – in some cases to none at all. Management's role is to create and communicate effective profit-improvement strategies, and to provide employees with the resources required to accomplish them.

To summarize, to create a true partnership with employees, employees must, just as owners do, accept some downside pay at risk. Incentive plans that provide employees market comparable pay, plus an incentive, do not create a true stakeholder employee group.

SECTION IV: MANAGING WITHIN A TOTAL PERFORMANCE SYSTEM

Chapter 16

Positive Leadership

Two approaches to management are discussed. Phase I of the Total Performance System continues the conventional compensation system, but adds performance scorecards and modest incentive pay opportunities. In Phase I, the manager changes from conventional management by perception and exception to positive leadership, and the management of objective, incremental improvement. In Phase II, below market salaries are augmented with above-market incentive pay opportunities. If the organization chooses to move toward this stakeholder pay system, the manager becomes a resource and coordinator for self-managed work teams.

What is Performance Management?

Applied behavior analysis is the scientific investigation of human behavior in applied settings. Human behavior occurs across time, and an effective analysis of it requires an examination of events that occur before and after a behavior occurs. Events that occur before a behavior are termed 'antecedents' and cue or prompt specific actions. Events that occur after a behavior are termed 'consequences' and determine whether a behavior will be more or less likely to occur again, through their effects as reinforcers or punishers. The following illustration describes these relationships.

To Improve and Maintain Employee Performance:

ANTECEDENTS
- Scorecard
- Weekly Meeting

BEHAVIORS
- Planning
- Execution
- Adjustment

CONSEQUENCES
- Feedback
- Recognition
- Incentive Pay

Employee performance is optimized when the manager ensures effective antecedents and consequences are operating in the work place. The manager may personally provide antecedents and consequences – as for example directions and praise. In other cases, the manager arranges the antecedents and consequences – as for example scorecards and incentive pay. The more arranged prompts, feedback, and consequences the manager develops, the less time the manager has to devote to direct supervision. Further, arranged antecedents and consequences provide more consistent and predictable influences on behavior than do those that require the personal intervention of the manager.

Antecedents and consequences work together. A manager who provides one without the other will not obtain the desired results. We have all seen the mother or father who exhorts their child to do this or that, only to find the child studiously ignoring them. Why is this? It is likely due to a failure to provide consequences that are contingent on the request. For example, if the parent says "clean up your room", and the child does so, what consequences follow? If the parent comments on how nice the room looks, or does not criticize the child if it is clean, the likelihood the child will follow the instruction again is increased. If, however, the child cleans the room and there are no positive consequences, then the likelihood the instruction will be followed again decreases. The best task lists and instructions without follow-up are ineffective over the long term.

The typical bonus pay plan is an example of the opposite situation–consequences, or at least post-performance rewards, without proper antecedents. Telling an employee they will share in profit improvements, even if the share is significant, fails to describe what they must do to improve the profits. For this reason, bonus plans often fail to produce any significant improvements for the organization. In some cases, they may even stimulate behaviors that are detrimental to the organization's long-term profitability.

Offering me a million dollars to perform brain surgery might inspire me to try–but I wouldn't want to be the patient! A frightening prospect is to create a highly motivated group of employees, in the absence of any well-thought-out strategy. In the Total Performance System, the performance scorecard describes each employee's, or employee team's, role in the organization's strategy through priority-weighted, objective performance measures. Without some system like this, any attempt at incentive pay will either be ineffective or counter-productive.

Four Management Styles.

Though it is impossible to neatly classify managers and supervisors into discrete categories, there are broadly four general approaches to management. These management styles are useful in analyzing how managers can work better with their employees and optimize employee satisfaction, commitment, and performance. The table below displays the four styles as a two-dimensional grid. The vertical axis is employee performance while the horizontal axis is employee satisfaction.

THE LEADERSHIP GRID

Employee Performance	Autocratic Management	Positive Leadership
	Absentee Management	Paternalistic Management

Employee Satisfaction

The absentee manager spends little time 'on the floor', fails to provide employees assistance and recognition to improve job satisfaction, and does not provide clear direction, feedback or meaningful positive reinforcement for getting the job done. The result is a poor-performing area with high absenteeism.

The absentee manager neither arranges, nor provides effective antecedents and consequences for employees.

The paternalistic manager is a 'people person' who is involved with employees and concerned about meeting their needs. However, this manager's emphasis is on employee satisfaction and retention, rather than the area's performance. Employees still fail to receive the direction and performance feedback they need to achieve the area's goals. The paternalistic manager attempts to provide positive consequences, without effective direction or feedback.

The autocratic manager is results-oriented, and provides specific direction and feedback. However, results are usually obtained through intimidation (negative reinforcement), private and public criticism, ridicule and other aversive techniques. As long as employees have nowhere else to go, this manager's area will meet its goals. The autocratic manager may provide effective antecedents, but relies heavily on aversive consequences.

The positive leader provides clear direction, consistent feedback and positive consequences for success. The Total Performance System provides managers the tools they need to apply this approach – monthly performance scorecards and trend charts, and an opportunity to share monthly in the profits of the organization if the scorecard performances are achieved.

Positive leadership can be applied in the absence of a formal performance system, but requires each manager to translate the organization's strategy to specific performance measures for their area, and to personally provide positive consequences such as recognition, time-off, and prizes. The Total Performance System provides the manager the framework within which positive leadership can be practiced, without the manager having to develop the antecedents and consequences.

Positive Leadership.

The management techniques of Positive Leadership are outlined in the previous ABC chart.

Antecedents. Positive Leadership begins with the performance scorecard. The positive leader fully understands each performance measure, its relationship to the departmental, divisional, and organizational measures, and the relationship of these measures to increased profitability and employee incentive payouts. The positive leader is effective in explaining the scorecard measures and rationales to her employees, and gaining the commitment of employees toward achieving the scorecard goals. Frequent review is important, and the positive leader will have a weekly, one-hour 'performance briefing' to review the measures, their impact on each higher level of the organization, and ultimately profit improvement and incentive pay.

Establishing the connections between scorecard performances, strategic objectives, profitability and performance pay is a critical component of Positive Leadership. The Positive Leader must be kept fully informed of these relationships by the organization to be effective in explaining them to his subordinates.

Tactical Improvement Planning. The team's performance on each measure is reviewed in the weekly performance briefing. A decision is made as to which measure's improvement would have the most impact on increasing the overall scorecard index and incentive payout. A 'tactical improvement plan' is developed for the targeted measure. The improvement plan must then be executed, reviewed weekly, and adjusted as needed.

Feedback and Positive Consequences. The relationship of performance pay to performance improvement should be consistently reviewed. However, this relationship is not immediate, nor totally under the control of the employees. Strategic improvements often rely on other areas and profitability is affected by a number of variables that are unrelated to the employee's success on achieving their scorecard goals. To overcome these issues, the positive leader will develop and administer more frequent, targeted feedback for employees. These techniques include the weekly meeting, wall charts, performance logs, and coaching sessions.

To bridge the gap between performance improvement and performance pay, the positive leader will provide immediate social recognition for improvements. This recognition can be a simple compliment, or praise for an improvement, or may be a more formal 'celebration' sponsored by the manager. Contests within the department should generally be avoided. Improvements should be judged against previous performance –like golf–rather than against other employees–like tennis. Creating competition within a department will harm employee cooperation and create conflicts.

The Total Performance System

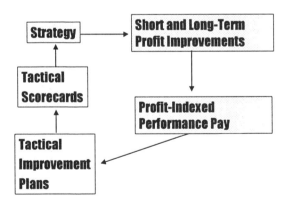

Creating Positive Leaders.

Antecedents. Developing positive leadership skills in managers follows the same principles as the ABC performance improvement model. The antecedents are, first, by example. The manager will have a scorecard and participate in the performance pay system. Positive leadership must also be practiced by senior managers in their relations with middle managers. This example provides a model for managers at each level of the organization. Second, a training program in positive leadership is the most efficient means for setting the stage for the implementation of a Total Performance System.

Behaviors. The senior manager should assist subordinate managers in improving their positive leadership skills. To do this effectively, the senior manager, or a performance manager trainer, must meet with managers, to help pinpoint improvement opportunities, and assist in developing tactical improvement plans. The improvement plan must then be executed, reviewed weekly, and adjusted as needed.

Consequences. The senior manager, or performance analyst, can attend some of the manager's performance briefings, and assess how effective they are at applying the principles with their employees in the meeting.

Managing Through Fear

Negative Reinforcement

Over the past 40 years, behavioral research has established that for rewards to be effective in increasing and maintaining performance, they must be delivered contingent on the desired performance. Salaries fail to meet this basic requirement. Salary payments are delivered according to the passage of some period of time, instead of delivery based on what employees have, or have not, accomplished. Yet, we all know intuitively that if there was no salary, the result would be absenteeism, tardiness, and minimal performance for most job positions. If this is so, then what is the relationship between salaries and employee performance?

You can get people to do things in two ways. You can reward them for finishing a task, or you can threaten them until they finish the task. The former is technically termed 'positive reinforcement' while the latter is 'negative reinforcement.' Examples of positive reinforcement are sales commissions, incentive pay, promotions, recognition, and praise. Many managers use positive reinforcement quite effectively.

The alternative management technique is to get people to work to avoid, or remove, undesirable consequences like criticism or loss of pay. This approach is referred to as 'negative reinforcement.' The principle of negative reinforcement is widely misunderstood, and often confused with punishment. This confusion arises from the use of aversive consequences for both punishment and negative reinforcement. However, we punish people to get them to stop doing something we don't want them to do, while negative reinforcement is used to get them to start, or continue doing the right things.

When an employee makes an error, or talks on the phone too much and the supervisor reprimands him, she is using punishment. When the supervisor tells an employee to complete a task by the end of the day – or – else, she is using negative reinforcement. The statement "Finish this report on time or you'll have to work on Saturday" is an example o f the use of negative reinforcement. Notice that only the 'promise' of an aversive outcome is made. The employee works to avoid the aversive outcome which, if he is successful, never occurs.

Because negative reinforcement operates through avoidance, the actual aversive consequences may never occur. In fact, when supervisors are really effective in the use of negative reinforcement (threats), the work does get done and the casual observer never sees the aversive control (the threats are never acted upon). "I have not said a cross word to an employee all year" may mean that employees are so terrified of the supervisor, they never present the opportunity for a reprimand.

Most supervisors and managers manage more through negative reinforcement than positive reinforcement. Why is this? Because management through positive reinforcement requires objective performance measures and frequent and consistent feedback regarding performance on these measures. To positively reinforce an employee's performance, you have to know the desirable behavior occurred. To tell people they are performing well once a year, isn't positive reinforcement. To tell people they are performing well in vague generalizations, isn't positive reinforcement.

There is a simple test to establish whether a manager is relying on positive or negative reinforcement techniques. Ask the supervisor what would happen to employee performance if he stayed home for two weeks. If he answers, "Nothing would get done!" then it is likely that performance is maintained through negative reinforcement. If the supervisor has to watch workers to make sure they perform, then they are working to avoid criticism and other adverse consequences that must be administered by the supervisor. Supervisors that rely on positive reinforcement, provide their employees objective measures and goals, consistent feedback, and incentives. The differences in employee performance and self-management in these two situations are dramatic.

Many managers believe wages and salaries are positive reinforcers. However, are employees really paid to work? Positive reinforcement must be 'contingent' on performance. When you perform well, you are reinforced and when you don't, you are not reinforced. Sales commissions are a good example of pay applied as positive reinforcement. The more you sell, the more you earn. Salary, in contrast, is only remotely related to day-to-day performance. The salary remains the same both in the amount and frequency of payment, as long as the employee performs at minimum standards.

Salaries ensure a minimum level of performance. But this is only true when the supervisor establishes and enforces the minimum level. Without supervisors, employees could conceivably perform no work at all, and still receive their salaries. It is the supervisor who translates the salary into performance contingencies. The two components work hand-in-hand. Without the salary, the supervisor would have little control. Without the supervisor, salary alone provides little control. Even with the salary, the supervisor is only effective if employees perceive the supervisor is capable of criticism, poor reviews, suspensions, and terminations.

Despite the absence of a day-to-day relationship between salary and performance, it could be argued that at least once a year salary increases serve as positive reinforcers. This is sometimes the case, but not the norm. Most organizations increase salary based upon inflation and the fact that another year has passed. Pay increases are expected by employees if they show up and perform at minimum standards. Due to this practice, workers are more concerned with not getting an increase than with getting one. As before, the threat of not getting a raise (negative reinforcement), is the management method more often than working to get an increase (positive reinforcement).

If an organization refuses to introduce performance measurement and performance pay, the management should at least learn to use negative reinforcement effectively. The following 'guidelines' for managing through fear are presented 'tongue-in-cheek' to illustrate the problems with using negative reinforcement as a management tool.

Guidelines for Effective Management Through Fear

There are two components in successful fear management—compensation and supervisor intimidation. Guidelines are provided for each component. Managed properly, these two components will ensure employees are adequately frightened to get a good day's work from them.

How to Use Compensation to Scare the Hell Out of Employees.

1. A high salary should be awarded to employees. All people spend to, or above, their income. High salaries make sure the employee will develop a high standard of living. The fear of losing this standard of living produces peak performance and inextricably binds the employee to the organization. As Casey Stengel once commented, "I like my ball players married and in debt, that way I know they'll play for me."

2. Hire people with dependent families. They have more to lose if terminated.

3. Hire older, less job mobile employees who have fewer job alternatives and must depend on their salaries for survival.

4. Introduce generous 'benefits' like health insurance and retirement plans. These encourage employees not to prepare for emergencies, and to become totally dependent on the good graces of the company.

5. Provide 'status' titles and perks when money is in short supply. To some people, loss of status is as frightening as the loss of cold cash.

6. Determine salary increases based upon tenure rather than performance. Most people realize it's a sure bet they will get older. By making a job seemingly secure, the employee becomes less able to deal with uncertainty and the threat of termination is enhanced.

How to Use Supervisors to Further Scare the Hell Out of Employees.

The two critical ingredients for a successfully intimidating supervisor are unpredictability and inability to be satisfied with employee performance. If these traits are mastered, the supervisor will be able to maintain consistent, high levels of employee anxiety, and therefore performance.

Unpredictability. This leadership quality is highly prized in organizations that manage through fear. Nothing enhances the maintenance of fear as much as putting quick-tempered, arbitrary people in control of an employee's livelihood. For fledgling supervisors, some suggestions for improving unpredictability are offered.

1. Interact with employees based on your mood – but not always.

2. *Occasionally publicly praise or promote an obviously inferior employee* to assert your absolute control over your employees' destiny.

3. *Conversely, publicly criticize your best performer for some insignificant infraction.* This action really confuses your subordinates.

4. *Fire someone.* Some random approach such as the 'termination dartboard' is best. Terminations should be unanticipated, and illogical, to produce the optimal level of fear in employees.

5. *Offer no goals or direction to your employees.* Or, offer a specific direction, and then change your mind once a week. Then criticize your employees for not getting the job done.

6. *Establish departmental goals and then write performance reviews on totally unrelated criteria.* Employees must be taught that your personal whim controls their destinies.

Unsatisfiability. Employees become complacent if they believe their performance, rather than your personal opinion, determines what happens to them. Nothing undermines your ability to intimidate your employees more than some smug high performer who thumbs his nose at you. To prevent this problem, follow these guidelines.

1. Never praise employees. They will begin to feel competent and comfortable in their jobs. As anxiety drops, so will your control over them.

2. To keep employees from getting the impression they are performing satisfactorily, *performance standards should not exist.* In this way, no matter how well an employee performs, he is kept completely in the dark and therefore anxious and productive.

3. Comment on performance errors only. Ignore competent performance and focus on criticizing deficiencies. An ideal opportunity to reinforce your authority is to raise hell over an error committed by a conscientious worker. This sets an example for others that you can never be satisfied, thus maintaining your ability to intimidate effectively.

Problems with Managing through Fear.

Though fear is an effective motivator, it carries with it several adverse side-effects that make positive reinforcement a more effective long-term management strategy. These adverse side-effects include:

1. Peer pressure is exerted to hold down performance to avoid supervisor demands for higher levels of performance.

2. Because the fear-driven workplace is unpleasant, employees avoid it through *tardiness and absenteeism.*

3. Employee turnover will increase proportionate to the use of fear as a management tool.

4. Threats and criticism produce anxiety that *may be counterproductive in highly skilled jobs or positions requiring customer contact.*

5. To use fear effectively, *there must be close supervision* which is expensive.

6. Since the supervisor is an adversary, she is *much less effective in coaching and assisting employees* in improving performance. Employees who lack skills will hide their deficiencies, rather than ask for help to correct them.

7. A fear-driven shop retards employee initiative and creativity. Constructive suggestions for improving performance will be withheld by employees.

8. Employees may strike back through constant complaining, work slowdowns, sabotage, theft, and law suits.

Advantages of Managing through Positive Reinforcement.

To manage through positive reinforcement, performance measures and goals must be defined; frequent feedback provided; and positive consequences applied for improvement or goal attainment. The advantages of this approach to management are:

1. Employees will work toward the goal rather than simply above the minimum standard.

2. Morale will increase and turnover and absenteeism will decrease.

3. Less direct supervision of employees will be required. Supervisors can spend more time forecasting, scheduling, coordinating, coaching and developing performance improvement plans.

4. An untapped resource will emerge. Given concrete objectives, feedback, and incentives, employees will show more initiative and creativity, and work with the supervisor to improve the unit's performance.

5. An organization that relies on positive reinforcement is not managed in the traditional sense. People share in the benefits of improving productivity, and work with each other on a more equal basis. *Over time, the manager – worker adversarial relationship is replaced with common goals.*

Chapter 17

Performance Analysis

The implementation of an objective performance measurement system enables an organization to conduct precise analyses of employee performance that pinpoint performance improvement opportunities. These analyses are invaluable in ensuring the accomplishment of an organization's strategy, and in optimizing profitability. Many of the performance measures will be 'lead' indicators that can prevent problems from becoming critical. This is value-added, since conventional financial indicators are typically 'lag' indicators. Furthermore, quantitative analyses can help an organization reduce ad hoc decisions in which opinions are often substituted for facts. This feature will help avoid the implementation of unnecessary or misguided programs.

There are five types of performance analyses: tactical, process, performance system, situational, and behavior component. Tactical analyses review the vertical relationship between scorecard measures and the organization's strategy. Process analyses review the horizontal relationships among behaviors and scorecard measures across departments. System analyses examine the relationships between the performance system scorecards, positive leadership and incentive pay, compared to the organization's human resource policies and procedures. Situational analyses examine the factors that restrict performance on the scorecard results measures. Behavior component analysis breaks down outcome measures into their behavior components to pinpoint deficient behaviors. Tactical, process, and system analyses should be conducted by the performance system administrator. Managers and their subordinates, or teams, usually perform situational and component analyses.

Tactical Analysis.

Since the 'Method of Cascading Objectives' was employed to design the scorecard system, each scorecard's measures should drive performances on the scorecard at the next higher organizational level. A simple logical review of the measures' relationships is usually sufficient to determine their causal relations. However, these relationships are sometimes ambiguous, and a more quantitative review may be required. To quantitatively examine the relationship between two scorecard measures, a graphic comparison is a straightforward approach.

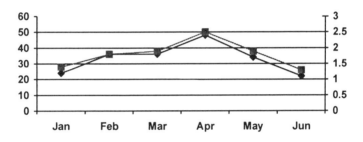

The preceding chart depicts a close relationship between the driver measure (cross-sell) and the results measure (sales). In some instances, the results measure may 'lag' the driver measure by one or more periods. The graph below depicts this situation.

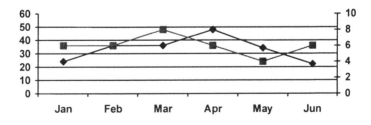

An alternative to graphic analyses are statistical analyses, such as correlational techniques.

To quickly review a total performance system's tactical validity, one interesting approach is 'cluster analysis.' This technique organizes measures in a graphic form based upon their intercorrelations. A performance measurement system, in which the measures were perfectly aligned, would display a cluster diagram similar to the one below.

Sample Measure Relationships Diagram

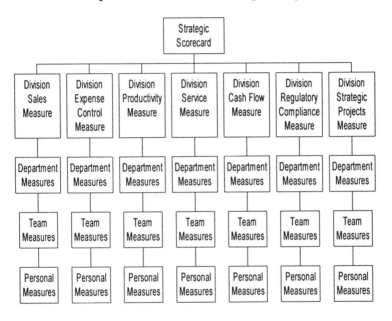

Process Analysis.

Tactical analysis examines the <u>vertical</u> relationships within the organizational hierarchy, especially as they relate to the overall organizational strategy. In contrast, process analysis examines the <u>horizontal</u> relationships across the organization, relative to workflow. The analysis examines the INPUT – PROCESS – OUTPUT relationships of an organization. These measures were referred to in the measurement design chapters as internal and external quality measures. Quality measures include three categories; timeliness, accuracy, and service style. A simple process analysis is illustrated below.

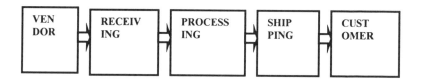

More complex workflow processes may involve loops and branches, rather than the simple linear relationship illustrated above. The objective of process analysis is to pinpoint weak points in the process chain, in terms of poor accuracy or quality, late arrival, and/or an undesirable service style. For example, the vendor could deliver the wrong materials, or deliver them late. These problems would, in turn, affect the entire process chain through delivery to the customer. An analysis of an organization's internal and external quality measures will pinpoint these critical problems. Process analysis, as described here, does not include improving the process or work methods. The purpose here is only to pinpoint breakdowns in the process chain, or to identify interdepartmental relationships that have not been adequately measured.

Performance System Analysis.

The performance system can be viewed in terms of the vertical alignment of performance measures, or the horizontal effectiveness of workflow processes. A third type of analysis, conducted by the performance systems analyst, examines the

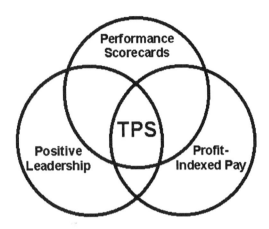

effectiveness of the three components of the performance system – scorecards, positive leadership, and incentive pay.

These analyses will be referred to as performance system 'audits', and discussed *in Chapter 18: Total Performance System Administration.* In addition to these analyses, a comprehensive performance system analysis would review the alignment of the measurement system with recruiting and selection practices, job training, performance reviews, promotions, merit increases, base compensation, benefits, and organizational communications.

Situational Analysis.

Situational analysis investigates the factors that influence a specific performance measure. From this analysis, as well as the behavior component analysis, a Tactical Improvement Plan (TIP) is designed to improve performance on the target measure. The decision tree below lists the critical issues in pinpointing the causes of low performance on a measure.

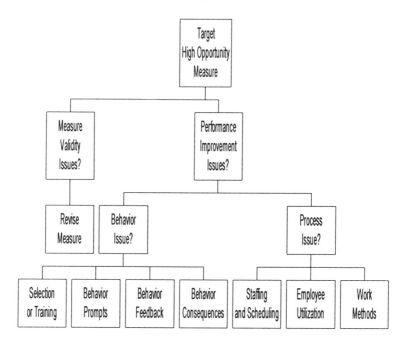

STEP 1: TARGET HIGH OPPORTUNITY MEASURE

Before developing a Tactical Improvement Plan (TIP), the manager or team must first decide which scorecard performance measure will be targeted. This decision is based upon a consideration of four factors:

1) The measure's priority weighting (consider high weights first)
2) The measure's current score (consider low scores first)

3) The measure's variability among performers & across time (consider high first)

4) The measure's trend (consider adverse or flat trends first)

The following is a mathematical method for helping an individual, or team, consider all four factors, to decide which performance measure to target for the development of a TIP. The measure weight and variability are rated high = 3, moderate = 2, low = 1. The percent gain is rated low = 3, moderate = 2, and high = 1. The trend percent is rated adverse = 3, flat = 2, and improving =1.

The sample data below are based on a scorecard for a restaurant shift manager.

Personal Sales – moderate weight (20%), high % gain (110%), moderate improving trend (3%) and moderate variability (10.5%).

Shift Sales Per Meal – moderate weight (20%), low % gain (25%), flat trend (.6%), and low variability (4.2%).

Shift Gross Margin % – low weight (10%), low % gain (20%), adverse trend (-2.2%), and moderate variability (12.3%).

Shift Meals Per Labor Hour – low weight (10%), moderate % gain (60%), moderate improving trend (6.7%), and high variability (18.1%).

Shift Average Customer Satisfaction – high weight (30%), moderate % gain (72.7%), flat trend (-.5%), and moderate variability (8.9%).

New Location Milestone - low weight (10%), high % gain (100%), flat trend (.1%), and moderate variability (13.9%).

If we apply the ratings on the previous page to the above information, we can construct a table like the one below.

MEASURE	PRIORITY WEIGHT	% GAIN	TREND %	VARIA BILITY %	OPP. SCORE
PERSONL SALES	2	1	1	2	4
SALES PER MEAL	2	3	2	1	12
GROSS MARGIN %	1	3	3	2	18
MEALS / LABOR HR	1	2	1	3	6
CUST SAT.	3	2	2	2	24
NEW LOCATN	1	1	2	2	4

The highest opportunity measure is customer satisfaction (24), followed by the gross margin percentage (18). The final test is which of these measures would require the least effort to improve.

STEP 2: MEASURE VALIDITY ISSUES

Before you begin looking for behavior or process improvement solutions, you should first examine the targeted performance measure's validity. If the measure is invalid, it should be revised or eliminated, rather than assigned a tactical improvement plan. Measure validity dimensions include:

Controllability – Can employees implement a change that will significantly affect the target measure? The measure level should be individual, small team or department.

Focus – Does the scorecard reduce focus on the target measure by containing too many other measures? Consider reducing the number of measures on the scorecard.

Priority – Is the target measure's priority weighting sufficient to ensure employees attend to the measure? Increase the target measure's weight to increase employee attention to the target measure and to increase reinforcement for improvement.

Base or Goal – The goal represents the organization's strategy, and generally should not be changed unless the strategy changes. If performance is consistently below base, consider lowering the base to the current performance level. If performance is consistently above goal, increase the goal, but only if the increase is required to meet organizational goals.

Some measure validity issues can be determined from a review of the measure's performance chart. These are presented below with example charts as illustrations.

    a. Poorly defined performance measure.
    b. Poorly defined or changed base or goal.
    c. Conflicting scorecard measures.

Each performance chart should present the measure's actual performance for six to twelve months, and the measure's base (original performance) and goal.

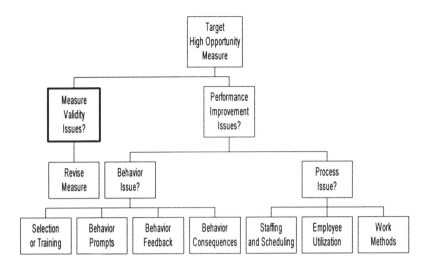

1. Measure Validity Issues: Zero Variability Measure

In this example, the performance measure is always at goal and exhibits almost no variability. The measure, as defined,

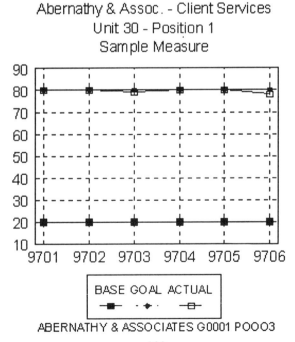

does not vary across time indicating it is not likely a valid performance measure. The measure will, then, not contribute additional improvement to the job position or organization. The measure definition may be a 'yes-no' that needs to be scaled across more increments, or the measure may be subjective. In other instances, performance has been improved and consistently remains at goal. In these cases, it is important to continue to reinforce goal performance, even if performance is consistently at, or above, goal.

2. Measure Validity Issues: High Variability

In this example, the performance is highly variable from month-to-month. This may be due to process problems, but when the variability is extreme it often indicates a poorly

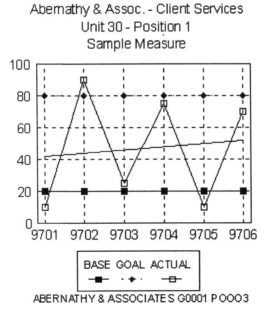

defined measure that is subject to large changes in the opportunity to perform. The measure may need to be redefined as a ratio of performance-to-opportunity or as a rolling average across months. In some cases, there will be only one or two high points that vary significantly from the average or trend. These may be examples of 'special' variability that represent temporary situations. Performance analysis should always relate to 'common' variability that results from recurring causes.

3. Measure Validity Issues: Poorly Defined Base

In this example, the base has been set too high. The result is that the measure has little or no effect on employee performance. The measure base should be set at, or somewhat below, current performance to reward incremental improvements in employee performance.

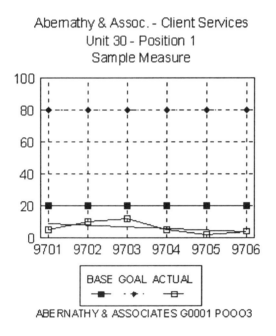

4. Measure Validity Issues: Poorly Redefined Goal

In this example, the goal was increased too quickly with a resulting decline in the performance trend.

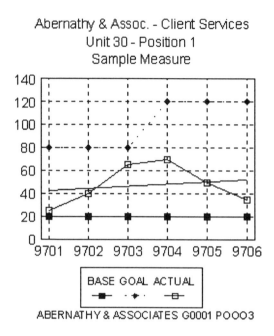

5. Measure Validity Issues: Conflicting Performances

The two measures may conflict. When one increases, the other decreases (e.g. productivity vs. quality). The logical relationship between them should be examined.

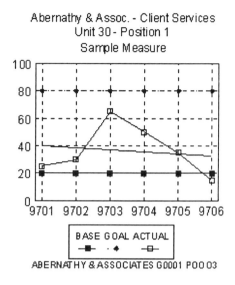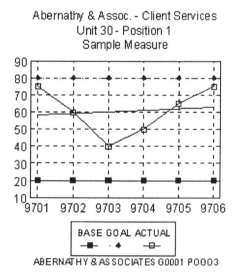

STEP 3: PERFORMANCE IMPROVEMENT ISSUES

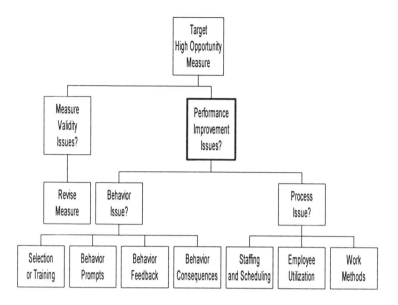

Behavior issues are reflected in charts with declining performances, high inter-employee variability, or increasing performance variability, with no change in work input variability.

Process issues are reflected in charts with either consistent low performance, or cyclic performance due to work input cycles that are not adjusted for in the employee staffing or work schedules.

STEP 4: BEHAVIOR ISSUES

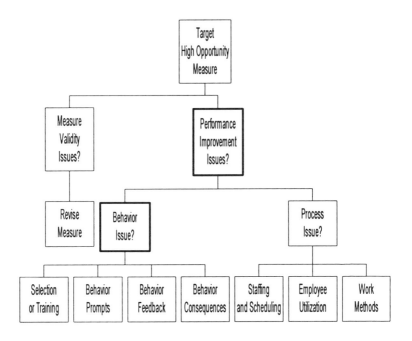

Selection or Training issues occur when employees have been selected that do not have the aptitudes for the job, or employees have been inadequately trained and lack the skills to do the job. Aptitude and pre-hire skills can be determined through testing. An exemplar (best performer) analysis can help determine what skills are needed to develop both training and selection programs.

Behavior Prompts are the cues, signals, instructions, job aids, labels, gauges, and other antecedents that inform employees of what action to take.

Behavior Feedback is information received by employees regarding their performance. Examples include scorecards, wall charts, coaching sessions, and others.

Behavior Consequences are what happens to employees as a result of performance including praise, recognition, feedback, added work assignments, criticism, and others.

Three chart analyses can assist in determining which behavior drivers are at issue. These are charts with:

1. High variability in performance among employees
2. Declining performance trends
3. Increases in performance trend variability

1. Behavior Issues: High variability among employees

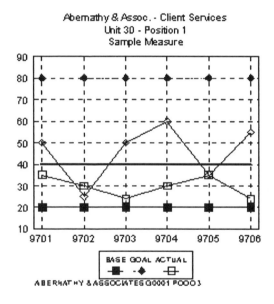

Training or aptitude issues are likely if:

There is a great deal of variability in performance on the measure among employees – the issue is likely aptitudes or training, since everyone presumably uses the same processes and receive the same prompts, feedback, and reinforcement.

New employees perform much lower than experienced ones, which suggests delayed or inadequate training.

High turnover in the area may indicate aptitude issues related to selection procedures.

Analyzing the behaviors of 'exemplar' or superior performers will give you an understanding of behaviors that may be constraining success for poor performers.

2. Behavior Issues: Declining Performance Trend

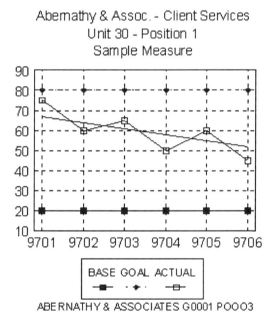

Declining performance trends indicate that behavior contingencies, rather than training or aptitudes, are the likely issue, since the employees performed better in the past.

Possible behavior contingency issues are:

> A reduction in directions, instructions, and guidance (prompts)
>
> Conflicting assignments
>
> A reduction in the quality or frequency of feedback
>
> Reductions in the performance pay opportunity or pay out
>
> Conflicting consequences such as criticism for failing to complete non-measured tasks, or poor performance reviews
>
> A change in managers may be the cause of the above problems

3. Behavior Issues: Increase in performance trend variability.

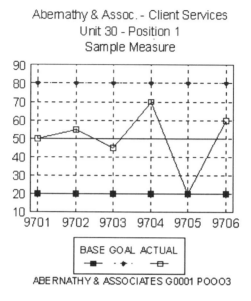

An increase in the month-to-month performance variability may be due to changes in work input, but often indicates behavior contingency problems. Possible causes include:

    Increased tardiness or absenteeism

    Excessive assignments to unmeasured tasks

    Inconsistent guidance and feedback

    Change in managers

Behavior Contingency Analysis and Observation Guide

To pinpoint which behavior contingencies are the root cause of the performance improvement opportunity, discuss the following items with employees, and then observe the job situation directly.

1) Does the employee have the skills necessary to perform at standard? (If yes, skip to item 3.)

2) If no, the issue is likely aptitudes or training.

3) If yes, has performance declined over time or have any prompting, feedback, or consequence changes occurred that might have affected performance?

Prompts. Are sufficient situational cues present to guide the performance? That is, does the employee know 'who, what, when, and where' the behavior is to occur?

Feedback. Is sufficient performance feedback provided in the situation? Can the employees accurately estimate how often the target behavior presently occurs? What percentage of the behaviors receives feedback? Is the feedback specific to the individual employee? What is the delay between the behavior and feedback? Is the feedback positive?

4) Does the feedback provide corrective action?

Consequences. Are the consequences for the behavior positive, predictable, immediate, and sufficient? Are there 'competing' contingencies that interfere with the target behavior or prevent the behavior from being reinforced?

5) What general solution to improve the target behavior does the employee suggest?

STEP 5: PROCESS ISSUES

Process issues can include staffing and scheduling, employee utilization, and work methods. There are two common chart analyses that suggest process problems:

Consistent low performance
Consistent performance cycles

Process Issues: Consistent Low Performance

Consistently low performance most likely suggests a process problem, such as improper staffing, late, poor quality input, or inefficient work processes. A similar data trend, however, can also be caused by poor, employee selection procedures or training.

Process Issues: Consistent Performance Cycles

If there are consistent cycles in performance, they are most likely due to changes in work input, with no corresponding correction in staffing or work scheduling. Solutions include flexible scheduling and cross-utilization.

Component Analysis

The final type of performance analysis is component analysis, in which a results measure's performance is subdivided into its behavioral components. Each component is reviewed to determine which component is constraining the overall results. Component analysis can be conducted for:

a. Sales
b. Productivity
c. Customer Service
d. Expense Control

Sales results (revenue or gross profit) are a function of four component behaviors; prospecting, closing, cross-sell, and up-sell. The measures are mathematically related, as illustrated in the formula:

Revenue = Prospecting x Closing x Cross-sell x Up-sell

For example, a salesperson's performance data for a given month are:

Prospects seen	=	100
% Prospects Closed	=	30%
Products per Sale	=	2.5
Revenue per Product	=	$60.00

The revenue for the month would be 100 x .30 x 25 x $60.00 or:

100 x .30 = 30 x 2.5 = 75 x $60.00 = $4,500

A comparison of the component behaviors to past performance, or the normative performance of all sales people, will pinpoint which component to target for improvement.

Productivity is a function of efficiency and utilization. Similar to sales, productivity can be mathematically stated as efficiency (processing speed) x utilization (percent time in production). For example:

Productivity   =   Efficiency   x   Utilization

75 units / hour =   100 units / hr x   75%

Utilization = prod hrs / actual hrs = 6 hrs / 8 hrs = 75%

Productivity can only improve, if either utilization improves with no reduction in efficiency, or efficiency improves with no concurrent decline in utilization. In other words, increasing efficiency without increasing input volume or decreasing staff, will not yield a productivity improvement.

Customer satisfaction components include service or product timeliness and quality, as well as service 'style'. Data for these components can be gathered from direct measurement, or from customer survey data. Though direct measurement is more accurate, it can be argued that customer perceptions are all that really count, and that survey data is therefore more useful.

Customer service timeliness may refer to response time, turnaround time, or deadline performance. Response time is the delay between a customer inquiry and the employee's acknowledgement in person, by phone, mail, or e-mail. Turnaround time is the delay between the receipt of work input and the final output. Deadlines are date driven service or product delivery agreements between the employees and the customer.

Turnaround time is affected by the area's productivity and work input quality. Productivity and turnaround time are mathematically related. Given a constant input volume, turnaround time decreases as productivity increases. The formula is:

Turnaround Time = Input Volume / Productivity Ratio

For example, an area's productivity is 100 units an hour. If the input volume is 500 units then it will require 500 / 100 = 5 hours to complete the input.

Performance to budget. It is a common practice to measure managers on their performance to an expense budget. To target actionable expenses for tactical improvement, two factors are considered. First, is a line item expense variable or fixed and second, is the expense under the discretionary control of employees.

In some cases, expenses deemed as fixed expenses could be converted to variable ones. For example, labor expense may be fixed (constant), when with proper scheduling, it could be made more sensitive to volume. Other convertible expenses include utilities, occupancy expense (where areas can serve shared purposes), and inventory.

Non-discretionary expenses can be converted to discretionary ones through empowering employees to make decisions concerning, for example, purchasing, maintenance, and inventory. The more discretionary control employees are given, the more impact their expense control tactical improvement plans will have.

Chapter 18

Total Performance System Administration

Performance Scorecard Analysis.

The illustration below is a sample screen from our "Data Viewer" performance system database. The scorecard system 'audit' is displayed. Six measures are used to evaluate the overall validity of an organization's scorecard system. These are complexity, focus, objectivity, alignment, controllability, and the performance index.

Performance Data Audit - System Audit

Company: Prime Rib House As of 13/17/97

Scorecard System | Performance Pay | Leadership

Validity Measurement	Current	Previous	% Change	Norm	% Norm
Complexity (Emps/Scorecard)	1.61	1.61	0.00	5.75	28.01
Focus (Meas/Scorecard)	3.89	3.89	0.00	4.78	81.38
Objectivity (Obj Meas / Tot Meas)	94.29	57.14	35.00	85.32	110.51
Alignment (Align Meas / Tot Meas)	100.00	100.00	0.00	88.51	112.98
Controllability (Meas*Lev/Tot Meas)	3.81	4.00	-4.84	3.53	108.01
Performance Index	46.96	43.35	8.85	52.76	89.00
Average % Norm					88.31

Overall Average % Norm 89.20

Print

Scorecard System Audit Measures.

1. Complexity. The scorecard system complexity is computed as the ratio of the number of employees, to the number of unique scorecards. A unique scorecard refers to a scorecard with a one-of-a-kind combination of scorecard measures. For example, an organization with 100 participating employees, and 10 unique scorecards, would have a complexity ratio of 100 / 10 = 10. There are an average ten employees assigned to each unique scorecard. The larger the complexity ratio, the simpler the system is to administer and analyze. For example, the simplest performance system would have all employees assigned to the same set of scorecard measures. The most complex system would have one unique set of scorecard measures for each employee.

2. Focus. Scorecard focus refers to the number of measures per scorecard. If a system has 100 measures and 10 scorecards, the focus ratio is 100 / 10 or 10 measures per scorecard. The fewer the number of measures per scorecard, the greater the focus and specific performances. However, focused scorecards, which have measures too distant from the performer, fail to balance measures, or provide inadequate coverage of all key job outcomes, are to be avoided. The total performance system focus should be computed as a weighted average, by multiplying each scorecard's number of measures by the number of assigned employees.

Example:

Measure Code	No. Measures	No. Employees	Weighted
1	5	10	50
2	7	20	140
3	3	100	300
Totals		130	490

490 / 130 = 3.76 measures per weighted scorecard

3. Objectivity. The percentage of total performance measures that employ quantifiable, numeric data. A test of whether a measure is truly objective is to ask whether two or more independent observers would arrive at the same data. Ideally, the objectivity goal is one-hundred percent. Subjective ratings should be avoided, with the important exception of customer perceptions of service quality. The average objectivity should be computed as a weighted average, by multiplying each measure by the number of assigned employees.

Example: (yes = 1)

Measure	Objective	Employees	Weighted
1	0	10	0
2	0	20	0
3	1	100	100
Totals		130	100

100 / 130 = 76% of the weighed measures are objective

4. Alignment. The percentage of performance measures that can be shown to drive, or influence, the organization's strategic measures. The decision as to whether a measure is aligned can be made logically or using correlational techniques. Ideally, every measure in the performance system should relate to the organization's strategy. However, it is unlikely that all job accountabilities are aligned, and therefore one-hundred percent alignment is not expected. The average objectivity should be computed as a weighted average by multiplying each measure by the number of assigned employees.

Example: (yes = 1)

Measure	Aligned	Employees	Weighted
1	1	10	10
2	1	20	20
3	0	100	0
Totals		130	30

30 / 130 = 23%

5. **Controllability.** This measure computes the average controllability of all the measures in the performance system. One way to describe controllability is in terms of a measure's organizational level. Levels will include personal (5), small team (4), departmental (3), divisional (2), and organizational (1). To compute overall controllability, multiply each measure by its level code and then by the number of employees assigned the measure. Sum these totals and divide by the total number of employees.

Example:

Measure	Level	No. Employees	Weighted
1	5	10	50
2	3	20	60
3	1	100	100
Totals		130	210

210 / 130 = 1.61

6. **Performance Index.** All of the employees' performance indexes (scores) are summed and averaged. A good range for the performance index is between 40 and 80 when the performance scale is from –20 to 100. If the average index is too low, employees will be discouraged and performance

improvement may be constrained. If the average index is too high, there will be little room for improvement.

Performance Pay Analysis.

The illustration below is a sample screen from our "Data Viewer" performance system database. The performance pay system 'audit' is displayed. Six measures are used to evaluate the overall validity of an organization's scorecard system. These are reliability, opportunity, payout, leverage, external equity, internal equity, and performance pay return.

Company: Prime Rib House — As of: 09/08/98

Scorecard System | Performance Pay | Leadership

Validity Measurement	Current	Previous	% Change	Norm	% Norm
Reliability (Changes / Scorecard)	N/A	N/A	N/A	N/A	N/A
Opportunity (Opp / Base Pay)	15.00	12.50	20.00	10.36	144.80
Payout (Payout / Base Pay)	7.20	5.42	32.84	6.05	118.93
Leverage (Mkt - Base Pay / Mkt Pay)	N/A	N/A	N/A	N/A	N/A
External Equity (Opp % / Leverage %)	N/A	N/A	N/A	N/A	N/A
Internal Equity (Hi Perf / Avg Perf)	0.67	0.66	1.52	0.69	97.76
PP Return (CNI / Payout)	N/A	N/A	N/A	N/A	N/A
Average % Norm					120.50

Overall Average % Norm — 105.73

Performance Pay System Audit Measures.

1. Reliability. This measure is computed as the average number of changes to scorecard measure definitions, bases and goals over a one-year period. Continual changes to scorecards will create unpredictability for employees, which reduces acceptance and improvement. Changes to scorecard measures also eliminate historical trends for those measures replaced. Our research finds a direct negative correlation between changes to bases and goals and performance trends – the more changes, the worse the trend. Priority weights, on the other hand, can be changed as new strategies and tactics dictate. The best policy is to review the entire system after six months, then annually thereafter.

2. Opportunity. Opportunity is computed by dividing the total incentive opportunity dollars by the total payroll. The optimal opportunity is difficult to determine because it is affected by a number of variables. These variables include:

• Market comparability – The value of an incentive opportunity is related to the employee's perceptions of how their base pay compares to pay in other organizations, or to other employees within the organization. If base pay is perceived to be below market, a higher opportunity is required to offset this inequity. Similarly, if the employee believes that more effort is involved in earning incentives, than in other jobs within the organization, a higher opportunity may be necessary.

• Risk – A general rule is that for every percentage point an employee is paid below market, there should be a three-percentage point above-market incentive opportunity. However, inconsistent opportunities, or scorecard performance constraints, may require a higher ratio.

• Consistency – A consistent opportunity will motivate performance more so than an inconsistent one. Budgeted (guaranteed) incentive opportunities are therefore more effective at lower opportunity levels than are profit-indexed ones.

• Performance Management – An organization whose managers consistently provide performance prompts, feedback, and social reinforcers will achieve higher performance gains than one that does not engage in effective performance management practices.

3. Payout. Payout is computed by dividing the actual total incentive payout by the total payroll. Payouts are affected by both the incentive pay opportunity, and scorecard performance. Ignoring the amount of incentive pay opportunity (see above), the issue is, then, the likelihood of a high scorecard score. Scorecard scores should fall between 40 and 80 for optimal results. If scores are too low, employees become discouraged. If they are too high, there is little motivation for continued improvement.

- Framing Effect – A troubling phenomenon is technically termed the 'framing effect' by behavioral researchers. When a goal is established, many employees perceive (correctly) that any score below goal reduces incentive pay. The incentives become a negative reinforcement system, rather than the intended positive reinforcement system. Employees are frustrated when they do not receive one-hundred percent scores rather than being reinforced by the additional pay earned for less than one-hundred percent performance. This effect is the proverbial 'half-empty – half-full' issue.

Commissions, piece-rates, and gainsharing do not suffer from this problem, since there is no goal in the payout calculation. However, such systems lack balance between measures, because an employee could choose to simply optimize one performance dimension at the expense of others. Further, it is difficult to maintain equitable risk-reward ratios across jobs with measures that are open-ended.

One solution is to reconfigure the scorecard 'conversion' scale such that 100 is not the upper limit or cap. The upper limit then becomes, for example, 130. The 100 score is considered goal-level performance while scores above 100 are considered beyond expectations. The argument against this approach is that employees will simply adjust their 'frame' to 130 over time. More research on this issue is needed.

• Payout Delay – A critical issue for incentive payout administration, is the delay of the payout with respect to the performance. Research finds that a delay of more than a few minutes, substantially reduces the effectiveness of a reinforcer. We have experimented with different payout delays and find that the shorter the delay, the more effective the incentive payment is in improving and sustaining performance. However, it is usually not practical to provide incentive payouts at the end of a day or shift. Fortunately, simply providing more immediate performance feedback will bridge the delay.

A second problem with delayed payouts, is that performances are typically totaled or averaged across the payout period. The longer the period, the less the payout relates to immediate performance. For example, in an annual payout scheme, an employee could perform well the first half of the year, but poorly in the second half. There would still be a payout but it would occur following a period of poor performance. Or, an employee could perform poorly during the first half of the year, and become discouraged because high performance the remainder of the year would not result in a maximum payout.

A final issue with payout delay, only relates to incentive systems in which employees are paid below market (leveraged) in exchange for higher incentive opportunities. In this situation, the incentive pay becomes a significant part of the base pay package. The employee needs at least monthly payouts to handle living expenses under this arrangement.

4. Leverage. Pay leverage is computed as market pay minus actual base pay divided by market pay. For example, a leverage percentage of 90% means that the employee's base pay is at 90% of market pay. Leveraged pay is an important issue for four reasons:

- Alignment – An employee cannot truly think and act like an owner without some investment and risk. Leveraging pay, creates a group of employees who think more like partners, or investors, than do employees paid a market-comparable salary.

- Motivation – Employees paid a market-comparable salary are usually satisfied with their pay. An incentive opportunity above market pay, may therefore provide little additional motivation to improve performance. Leveraged pay does not allow the employee this option. Poor performers will either improve their performance, leave the organization, or adjust to the lower pay.

- Pay Opportunity – Indexing a portion of pay to profits allows the organization to increase employees' total pay in proportion to the growth in net income. Guaranteed wages and salaries cannot be increased proportionate to profit increases since they will remain high when the organization may later experience a profit decline.

- Job Security – Fixed cost wages and salaries place the employee at risk during business downturns. Particularly in high labor cost businesses, the only option during low revenue periods may be a layoff. In contrast, leveraged pay reduces every employee's pay during downturns. As a result, the need for layoffs is postponed or eliminated.

5. **External Equity.** External equity is the equity of an organization's total pay system compared with other organizations who compete for the same employees. It is computed

as the opportunity % (2) divided by the leverage % (4). As mentioned previously, for every percentage point the base pay is below market, incentive pay should provide an opportunity to earn three percentage points in incentive pay (an external equity ratio of 3.0).

For example, if the incentive pay opportunity is 30% above market and the leverage percent is 10% below market (90%), then the external equity is 30% / 10% = 3.0. Organizations with high, consistent earnings may be able to offer a lower ratio successfully. Organizations that have a history of modest profits, or highly erratic profits, may need to increase the ratio beyond 3.0.

6. Internal Equity. Internal equity is the pay equity within an organization. The internal equity is computed by pay grade. Employees within each pay grade are ranked according to their performances (assumes scorecard measures are based on personal and small team performance). The average total pay of the top 15 percent is compared to the average pay of the bottom 15 percent. The formula is:

(Avg high pay/Avg low pay) / (Avg high score/Avg low score)

For example:

Avg high score = 90%   Avg high score pay = $2,000
Avg low score = 60%   Avg low score pay = $1,800

Therefore:

(2,000 / 1,800) / (90 / 60) = 111% / 150% = 74% internal equity ratio

Perfect equity would be 100% while percentages below 100% indicate inequity favoring low performers. Percentages above 100% indicate inequity favoring high performers.

7. **Performance Pay Return.** Return on performance pay is computed by dividing net income over threshold by total incentive pay. If the profit-indexed system described in this book is employed, the return should equal or exceed the original "share percentage" used to develop the incentive pay multiplier scale. The percentage return will usually exceed the original share percentage, due to unearned incentive opportunity created by scorecard performance adjustments.

Leadership Analysis.

The final audit component of the total performance system is leadership or management practices. Leadership practices are assessed in terms of specific manager behaviors as well as expected outcomes.

The illustration that follows is a sample screen from our "Data Viewer" performance system database. The leadership 'audit' is displayed. Six measures are used to evaluate the overall performance of an organization's leadership. These are tactical improvement plans, leadership survey score, performance trend, performance variability, and high performer retention.

Performance Data Audit - System Audit

Company: Prime Rib House   As of 12/17/97

Scorecard System	Performance Pay	Leadership				
Validity Measurement	Current	Previous	% Change	Norm	% Norm
Tactical Imprv Projs (TIPs / Scrcrd)	0.20	0.22	10.00	0.31	70.97
Leadership Survey (Average)	4.80	5.40	12.50	8.21	88.98
Performance Trend (Slope / Intercept)	1.23	1.24	0.81	1.51	82.11
Performance Variability (SD / Mean)	32.30	29.40	12.07	27.60	85.45
Hi Perf Retention (Low+Hi Attrition)	50.50	50.00	0.99	32.20	63.78
Average % Norm					92.59
Overall Average % Norm					98.20

Print

Leadership Audit Measures.

1. Tactical Improvement Plans. Tactical improvement plans are the 'engine' that drives organizational performance improvement. Ideally, the manager should meet with her employees one hour a week. During these meetings, improvement opportunities are identified, and an improvement plan is developed to capitalize on the opportunity. As described previously, these plans can be categorized broadly as behavioral or process improvements.

TIP's (tactical improvement plans) per scorecard is the indicator used to assess whether the organization's managers and employees are actively involved in the design and implementation of improvement plans. An ideal ratio would, of course, be 1.0. That is, one improvement plan has been implemented for each unique scorecard. A more realistic goal is typically 20% to 40%.

2. Leadership Survey. A leadership survey is used to determine if effective performance practices are being used by managers. Every six months, employees are asked to rate their supervisor on a list of key management practices. This survey is more of a 'lead' indicator than the other indices in the leadership audit. However, improvements in survey results should not be considered equivalent to true system results.

3. **Performance Trend.** This indicator assesses the overall average improvement across all scorecard measures in the organization. To compute this trend, raw performance data must be converted to standard scores and aggregated. This procedure is beyond the scope of this book. Our research finds an average first year trend of 2.75% gain a month or 33% over the course of a year. The first year, standard score trend for 2,195 scorecard measures, across eighteen organizations, is presented below.

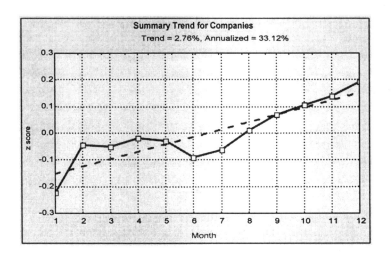

6. **Performance Variability.** This indicator assesses the overall performance variability across all scorecard measures in the organization. This procedure is also beyond the score of this book. The ideal variability would be one that collapses around a steadily improving trend line.

7. **High Performer Retention.** Effective leadership, performance measurement, and incentive pay should reduce high performer attrition. The high performer retention ratio is computed as the low performer attrition percentage divided by the high performer attrition percentage. For example, if the low performer (lowest 15% scores) attrition percentage is 15%, and the high performer (top 15% scores) is 10%, then the ratio is 15%/ 10% = 150%. Any ratio in excess of one-hundred percent, states that high performers are leaving at a slower rate than low performers.

Performance System Administrative Structures

Three approaches to the administration of a Total Performance System are possible. The administration can be decentralized and left up to line management exclusively. The administration can be centralized as a staff or outsourced function, or the administration can be conducted by a TPS committee.

• **Line management administration** allows each manager to determine, within a set of organization-wide guidelines, the scorecard measures, bases, goals, and the priority weights. This approach is cost-effective since no staff or committee is required. Each manager is responsible for tracking performance data and providing reports to employees – typically using spreadsheets or simple databases. The incentive opportunities should be assigned to an executive group, or the Human Resources department.

• **Staff administration** uses one or more staff employees to administer the system. This approach ensures that all scorecards are aligned with the strategy, provides for equity and continuity across scorecards, and enables the organization to conduct an organization-wide analysis of the system's validity and performance.

- **Committee administration** assigns managers and employees to an oversight committee. All proposals to change the system are reviewed by this committee. This approach is fairly cost-effective and provides an organizational perspective to the management of the system.

Generally, the professional staff management is the most effective, if the organization can afford it. The committee approach is next best, with the decentralized approach being the least effective due to distinct differences in manager and supervisor interests or skills in measure definition, goal setting, and monthly administration. Combinations of these three approaches are also possible.

Administrative Procedures

The following are sample procedures for the Total Performance System. The list is not exhaustive.

Will there be:

Data collection forms	Yes	No
Personal performance data	Yes	No
Team performance data	Yes	No
Internal customer survey data	Yes	No
Leadership survey data	Yes	No
Team peer survey data	Yes	No
Forms submitted to reporting coordinator by:	_____	
Scorecards distributed by:	_____	
Performance payroll distributed by:	_____	

Will the incentive pay percentage be based upon personal pay?

Yes   No

Will incentive pay be listed as a field on the standard payroll check or as a separate check _____?

Monthly team meetings	Yes	No
TIPs submitted to coordinator	Yes	No
Six-month leadership survey	Yes	No
Scorecard revisions due by:	_____	
Six-month performance audit due by:	_____	

Ensuring Scorecard Validity

Do not revise scorecards:

- only because scores are low
- because a measure is not 100% controllable
- because opportunity varies
- because data has to be collected
- through negotiations

Do revise scorecards to:

- align measures with organizational goals
- reduce subjectivity
- increase employee control over measure
- reduce the number or complexity of measures
- simplify data collection

Scorecard revision policies and procedures

Who can revise a scorecard? _____

What can be revised? _____

When are revisions submitted? _____

To whom are they submitted? _____

Manager Success Factors

Studies of successful managers in the Total Performance System consistently find they, and their employees, have above average performance scores and performance pay earnings. These factors are:

1. Scorecards are revised only when absolutely necessary. This practice makes the system predictable and reliable for employees.

2. Employees fully understand the scorecard and performance pay calculations and their relation to organizational profitability and goals.

3. Performance feedback is provided by the manager throughout the month – not just when the scorecards are distributed.

4. Scorecards are distributed at team meetings. Results are discussed, improvement opportunities identified, and results improvement plans are designed and implemented.

5. The manager consistently applies Positive Leadership skills.

Performance System Procedures and Policies

The policies and procedures for the Total Performance System are as follow:

Administration Procedures.

Performance data is submitted to the Performance System Coordinator by the _____ of each month.

Data will be transmitted for processing by the _____ of each month.

Scorecards and payouts will be verified, approved, and transmitted by the _____ of each month.

Scorecards will be distributed by the _____ of each month.

Performance pay will be distributed by the _____ of each month or in the _____ payroll check.

Scorecard Revision Procedures (includes new scorecards).

Revisions must be approved by _____.

Revisions may only be submitted by _____.

Revisions must be submitted to the coordinator by _____.

Employee Status Change Procedures.

Changes in employee scorecard assignments (job positions) or base pay must be submitted to the coordinator by _____ to be effective in the next reporting period.

Changes in employee status are effective _____.

Performance Pay Procedures.

Employees' performance pay bases are reviewed and revised _____.

Exceptions to this policy are:_____

The criteria for an employee basis change are: _____.

The Controllable Net Income, Multiplier Threshold, and Multiplier Scale will be reviewed and possibly revised _____.

The criteria for a change in the Multiplier computations are: _____.

Performance Pay Eligibility Requirements.

Current employees. _____

New Employees. _____

New employees will participate in the performance pay system when _____.

Employee Compliance Requirements.

Employees who attend work less than ____ percent of a reporting period are ineligible for performance pay that period.

Employees who receive unacceptable performance reviews will be ineligible for performance pay for _____.

Terminated employees will receive performance pay _____.

Reporting Compliance Requirements.

Failure to report performance data on time results in_____.

Failure to report accurate performance data results in_____.

Falsification of performance data results in _____.

No right or interest of any participant in the performance pay system shall be assignable or transferable.

Obstacles to the Implementation of a Total Performance System

Over the past twenty years, we have assisted a diverse group of organizations in the implementation and administration of Total Performance Systems. From these experiences, we have encountered many potential obstacles that can undermine a successful application. The following section describes these obstacles and strategies for overcoming them.

Design Obstacles.

1) Expertise. When an organization's management has legal problems – they consult an attorney. To install new computer hardware or software–they consult M.I.S. professionals. For complex tax and financial issues–they consult an accountant. But when this same management group designs a performance system, they often believe that no special knowledge or skills are required.

Is there anything really worth knowing about behavior and behavior systems that an intelligent person doesn't already know from personal experiences? Aren't we all experts in human behavior? There are three reasons personal experiences, alone, are not sufficient for the design of performance systems. First, personal experiences are necessarily limited. Few individuals have managed behaviors in a sufficiently wide variety of contexts to arrive at fundamental performance management principles. Second, personal perceptions may significantly color our assessment of causes and outcomes in the absence of hard data. Finally, every individual seeks the simplest, least-effort solution to a problem. Without data that prove an approach to be effective or ineffective, the easiest solution will always prevail.

The academic and scientific communities are also to blame. When a new medical procedure or drug is proposed, we wait for a scientific evaluation before we use them. However, anyone with a word processor can become an instant expert in human behavior. Few theories or practices are subjected to rigorous review. Before implementing new training or management programs, the skeptical manager should always ask – show me the data!

Fortunately, there is a body of knowledge that has been developed from careful experimentation. The field of Applied Behavior Analysis provides a solid foundation for anyone tasked to design, implement, and manage performance systems. Some of the findings are counterintuitive, and some of the findings challenge our personal beliefs. Nevertheless, the principles and techniques have been rigorously tested in both laboratory and applied settings. The application of these principles yields consistent results that are well worth engaging expertise or learning the principles.

2) Complexity. A common criticism of a total performance system is that it is too complicated. A performance measurement system, however, simply reflects the actual complexity of an organization. If an organization has only a few job positions, products, and services, the performance system will be simple. However, if the organization has many unique job positions and work outputs, the system will be more complex.

A common error is to apply a simple measurement system to a complex organization. For example, all business organizations produce a net income. Profit sharing relies on this single measure of an organization's performance. Nevertheless, net income is an outcome – not a performance. It is a results, not a tactic or strategy. You cannot directly improve net income (with the exception of some accounting adjustments). You have to improve sales, expense control, customer retention, productivity and the like, which then, in turn, improve the net income. To improve these net income 'drivers', measures must be installed at the level the performance occurs.

3) Frequency. Many organizations measure and reinforce performance on an annual basis. Examples are annual performance reviews, annual profit sharing, annual bonuses, and annual gainsharing. One common argument for this practice is that the organization's performance can only be assessed at the end of the year. If we evaluate performance or pay incentives during the year, employees could receive good evaluations or incentive payments even when the end-of-year results are poor.

This focus on annual results probably stems from the fact that taxes and other events occur annually. But an organization earns and spends money every day. Annual data is totally inadequate as a performance management tool. Furthermore, it takes at least three data points to determine the trend of a performance. Annual reporting would inform us of a trend only every three years. Quarterly reporting still requires nine months before a problem is addressed, or to determine if an initiative is working.

When you consolidate data over time, you only see the cumulative or average performance. An effective performance analysis, however, examines performance variability to pinpoint problems and successes. Annual data are always 'lag' indicators – never 'lead' indicators. Lead indicators allow management to address a problem before it becomes serious or intractable. For example, we could measure pilot safety by the number of airplane crashes each year. This is an example of a lag indicator and would, of course, be unacceptable. Better to measure pilot safety behaviors on each flight or a sample of flights. These measures are preventative. The same holds true for business metrics.

Monthly performance data reporting is usually sufficiently frequent to provide for timely analyses, and to provide employees timely enough feedback that they can adjust their performances quickly. In some cases, monthly feedback is not adequate for pinpointing problems. In these instances, ad hoc local measures can be installed to achieve optimal time intervals to maximize performance. These time intervals may be weekly, daily, end-of-shift, end-of-job, or even hourly for high frequency behaviors, like data entry or other types of production jobs.

4) Reporting Format. Many organizations, especially regulated ones, collect a good deal of data. In these instances, the issue is how often the data is compiled and reported, and who receives it, more so than the volume of data collected. Another issue may be the way the data is reported. As Kaplan and Norton have pointed out, many organizations segment their reporting so that financial, productivity, service, project management, and other measures reside in different databases; are reported at different intervals; and are sent to different audiences. The consequence may be that unbalanced decisions are made. For example, if I only look at productivity data, I may make staffing adjustments that adversely impact service, safety, or other critical issues. The balanced performance scorecard reporting format ensures that all interrelated results appear on the same report.

5) Group Plans. There are two reasons for the popularity of group plans – they are easier to design and manage than small team or personal plans, and there are some who believe group plans promote cooperation. A group of one hundred employees would require only one set of measures (scorecard) while team plans could create up to ten or more scorecards. This is an effort-reward issue. Our findings, and many others, find that the more control an employee has over a measure, the greater the performance gain. Even without research support, common sense tells us that we can usually influence a small team or personal performance measure more so than a group measure.

The assumption that group plans will spawn cooperation remains unproved. In fact, group plans may have the opposite effect where there are significant differences in performance within the group. Since group plans pay everyone equally, the poor performer receives the same payment as the high performer. High performers will find this unfair, which may create more, rather than less, tension in the group. Economists have written extensively about the 'free rider' problem in socialism and other group-based economic schemes.

Implementation Obstacles.

1) Manager Training. The most significant implementation obstacle is inadequate manager preparation and training. If the manager doesn't understand the system, or fails to buy into the system, then it will likely fail with the manager's subordinates. As an extreme example, on more than one occasion we have discovered managers who refused to distribute scorecards or talk about them. On further investigation, the issue was almost always the fact the manager did not understand the system and was avoiding embarrassment. Perhaps a worse situation, is the manager who distributes the scorecards, but gives his employees inaccurate information regarding their purpose or calculations.

2) Communications. A formal orientation for employees is critical to the successful implementation of a Total Performance System. The need for good communications increases with the distance the performance measures are from direct employee control. That is, profit sharing requires a better communications program than department level measures. Team and personal measures require less communication than department measures.

3) Establishing the pay–performance connection. A very common employee response to various performance pay plans, is to view the plan as equivalent to a lottery. When a pay out occurs, that's great. When it doesn't, that's too bad. In either case, the employee perceives he has little control over the outcome.

We recommend that performance improvement planning should occur in the initial orientation meeting. Once the system is explained, the manager or trainer immediately begins working with employees to pinpoint improvement opportunities for which improvement plans are created. This approach firmly establishes the link between performance improvement, increases in performance scores, and increases in performance pay.

4) Payouts. A bad precedent is when the first performance reports and incentive payments are late, inaccurate, or too low. The reporting process accountabilities and deadlines should be in writing. Many organizations avoid these problems by conducting a three-to-six month 'dry-run' in which reports and potential payments are distributed, but no money is paid. The dry-run should not be too lengthy, because employees may lose interest; initial improvements may not be properly recognized; and the reporting procedure may still be lax, since there are no serious repercussions for late or inaccurate reporting. If the incentive pay potential is linked to profits, care should be taken to either introduce the system during a time period when payout opportunity exists or, 'seed' the program with a modest guaranteed incentive opportunity for a pre-defined period of time (3-6 months).

Administration Obstacles.

After the program is up and running, there are mistakes and oversights that create obstacles for optimal improvement.

1) Scorecard changes. Many managers or administrators cannot resist constant tinkering with the scorecard system. Our research finds a direct, negative relationship between the number of changes made to a scorecard and the performance improvement on the scorecard measures (the more changes, the less improvement). This natural tendency can be countered by simply adding a committee or other third party review for all proposed scorecard changes. After the system has matured, changes can be introduced on an annual basis.

2) Absence of Improvement Planning. We find a direct and significant correlation between improvement planning and performance improvement. Those companies whose managers meet weekly, or monthly, to review scorecard results, and to design improvement plans, obtain much higher improvements. Employee enthusiasm and commitment for the system also increases when frequent meetings and plans are a part of the process.

3) Employee Empowerment. Personal and small team performance measures that directly share profits with employees empower employees. To receive personal recognition and increased pay, the employee no longer has to wait for the annual review, nor guess what the supervisor's ratings will be. In this new context, employees are often more proactive and assertive than under conventional management systems. Managers, who fail to adapt to this new situation, will restrict both performance improvement and employee satisfaction with the system.

4) System Perspective and Evaluation. Too often there is no one in the organization responsible for monitoring the overall system validity and impact on a continuous basis. Rather, each manager personally evaluates, and often modifies, the system from a restricted local view. Over a period of time, this piecemeal perspective can do great damage to the integrity of the original cascading objectives system. The incentive pay will no longer drive strategy and cooperation among departments. Further, the pay equity will decline as goal setting and measure selection become local, rather than organizational decisions.

Chapter 19

An Analysis of Twelve Organizations' Total Performance Systems

The first twelve months' results of twelve organizations' performance scorecard and incentive pay systems are analyzed. All the organizations distribute monthly performance scorecards to their employees, which were provided by Abernathy & Associates' outsourced administration service. The twelve were selected from a total reporting group of thirty-five companies. The selection requirements were that the organization had reported 15 consecutive months, and had a database in which the measure types were coded to allow for the analysis.

Six of the organizations experienced statistically significant overall performance improvements, four yielded no significant change, and two experienced a decline in performance. The key variable clusters affecting performance change were found to be scorecard design and administrative variables, incentive pay variables, and organizational structure variables. The most important organizational success variable was the implementation of scorecard measures that employees could directly influence.

The table below describes the organizations by industry type, number of employees and the number of performance measures.

Company	Type	No. Employees	No. Measures
A	Manufacture	286	179
B	Retail	62	61
C	Manufacture	348	39
D	Banking	464	18
E	Publishing	66	54

F	Distribution	206	228
G	Banking	747	536
H	Banking	186	94
I	Distribution	99	56
J	Banking	1140	618
K	Distribution	148	75
L	Manufacture	537	237
ALL		4289	2195

Each organization's performance scorecard system was developed using the method of 'cascading objectives'. An organizational 'strategic scorecard' was first designed, and served as the 'blueprint' for scorecards at successively lower levels of the organization. A scorecard could be assigned to an individual, team, or department. Scorecard measures could relate to data from an individual performer, a team, or group. Therefore, a given scorecard could consist of team measures, individual measures, or a combination. The format of the performance scorecard was common to all companies. Each employee received a scorecard for the month's performance in the following month. The scorecard components were:

Base – The measure data point that represents zero on the performance scale. Typically, it is defined as current or minimally acceptable performance.

Goal – The measure data point that represents one-hundred percent performance. Typically defined as one standard deviation above the mean or as required to achieve higher level goals.

Conversion Scale – The scorecard has an eleven-interval scale that spans from –20 to 100%. The last two intervals are larger to increase the payout as the performer nears goal. The measure data are converted to a 'percent gain' using the formula (actual – base) / (goal – base) and then interpolated on the scale (scores are rounded down). The scale interval in which the percent gain falls is termed the performance score.

Priority Weight – The weight is a percentage. The sum of the percentage weights always sums to one-hundred percent. The weight represents the measure's priority relative to the organization's strategic priorities.

Weighted Score – Each measure's performance score is multiplied by its weight to compute the measure's weighted score.

Performance Index – The weighted scores are summed to compute the overall scorecard performance index. The index percentage is multiplied by each month's incentive pay opportunity percentage to compute incentive payouts.

Data Collection Procedures

Performance measures were restricted to only measures in which the formula and data remained constant over the 15-month study period. Performance data were collected monthly for a fifteen-month period. The first three months were excluded from the study due to typical inaccuracies in reporting and changes in scorecard parameters when the system is first introduced. This decision to improve the accuracy of the study data by excluding the first three months, likely reduced the overall performance trend improvements, since performance in these months was often at its lowest level.

Each performance measure's data were gathered from either direct extracts from the organization's internal databases, or from manually entered data collected by managers and supervisors. Each month's data were transmitted to Abernathy & Associates early in the next month. Data were verified through a series of audit reports and corrected as required. Employees received their scorecards and incentive payments in the third or fourth week of the following month.

Descriptions of Analysis Variables

Variable	Description
Company	Companies are assigned an I.D. from A-L.
Employees / Scorecard	The ratio of employees to unique scorecards. The ratio is considered a measure of the organization's scorecard 'system focus'.
Measures / Scorecard	The ratio of performance measures to unique scorecards. The ratio is considered a measure of 'scorecard focus'.
Performance Index	The sum of the weighted measures percent gains on a scorecard. This index is the employee's score and determines the employee's incentive payout.
Team / Individual	Team refers to measures to which two or more employees are assigned to the same scorecard and thus receive the same score.
Average Weight	The average priority weighting assigned to a measure. Weightings determine a measure's contribution to the overall performance index and always sum to 100%.
Base Changes	A measure's scorecard base is the scale value that equals zero percent gain. The number of changes to the base value over 12 months is reported.
Goal Changes	A measure's scorecard goal is the scale value that equals 100 percent gain. The number of changes to the goal value over 12 months is reported.
Weight Changes	The number of changes to the priority weight over 12 months is reported.
Hourly / Salaried	The exempt or non-exempt status of employees reporting on a measure.
Guaranteed Opportunity	The percentage of an employee's base pay that is a fixed or guaranteed incentive pay

	opportunity. This percentage is multiplied by the employee's scorecard performance index to compute the incentive payout for the month.
Total Opportunity	The percentage of an employee's base pay that represents the total incentive pay opportunity. This percentage is the sum of guaranteed opportunity plus profit-indexed opportunity.
Payout	The actual opportunity multiplied by the employee's assigned scorecard's performance index.
Measure Type	Measures are classified as sales, expense control, productivity, regulatory compliance, quality, customer service, and projects.
Score	The scorecard scale conversion for a measure's data.
Trend	The dependent variable for the study. All raw data were converted to 'z' scores to allow for comparisons. The slope of the 12-month trend line was then computed and the sign adjusted to reflect whether the slope direction was an improvement (+) or a decline (−) in performance.

Issues Addressed in the Analysis

Scorecard Design and Administration Issues:

1) Does performance improvement differ among the types of performance measures (sales, customer service, quality, productivity, expense control, regulatory compliance, or projects)?

2) Do team or individual scorecards yield the most performance improvement?

3) Do hourly employees respond more to the system then salaried employees?

4) Does the 'system focus' (employees per scorecard) of the system increase improvement?

5) Does the 'focus' of the individual scorecards (measures per scorecard) increase performance improvement?

6) Does the priority weight assigned to a measure affect performance improvement?

7) Does the level at which a measure's base or goal is set affect performance improvement?

8) Do frequent changes in a measure's base, goal, or weight affect improvement?

Incentive Pay Issues:

9) Does the level of incentive pay opportunity affect performance trend?

10) Does the amount of incentive payout affect performance trend?

Table 3: Summary of Performance Trends

Company	Number of Measures	Trend Mean	Trend S.D.	95% Confidence Limit
A	179	+.0266	.1230	Yes
B	61	-.0026	.1048	Yes
C	39	+.0125	.1119	No
D	18	-.0251	.1415	No
E	54	.0015	.1267	Yes
F	228	-.0013	.1120	No
G	536	.0383	.1128	Yes
H	94	+.0304	.1164	Yes
I	56	-.0106	.1211	Yes
J	618	-.0011	.1245	No
K	75	+.0279	.1246	Yes
L	237	+.0256	.1436	Yes
ALL	2195	.0158	.1226	Mixed

Exceptions. Company A's results are from four small plants in four different locations. Company F's results are from two primary locations. Company G is the retail portion of a bank while company H is the 'back office' of the same bank. Company J represents a holding company consolidation of several smaller banks. Company L results are from six primary locations. Company L did not implement an incentive pay program. Only company L provided formal performance management training to their supervisors and managers.

Comparison of Significant Trends for Each Company

Chart 1 is a comparison of the trends for the eight companies' with statistically significant trends.

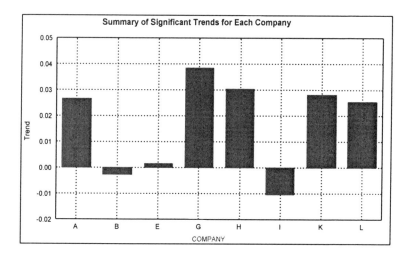

Chart 2. The overall trend for the eight companies with significant trends was .0276.

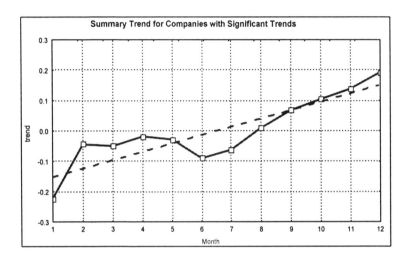

Results for Each Company

Chart 3. The overall performance trend for all twelve companies' 2,195 measures, and 4,289 employees, was computed for months 1-12. The average trend (slope) was .0158.

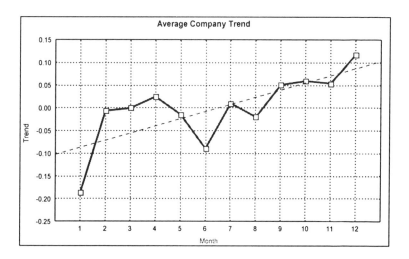

Chart 4. Company A is in manufacturing with 286 employees and 179 small team and individual performance measures. The trend was significant with an increase of 2.66% per month.

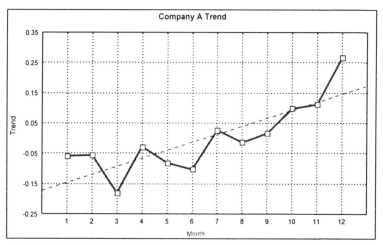

Chart 5. Company B is in retail with 62 employees and 61 small team and individual performance measures. The trend was significant with a decrease of -.26% per month.

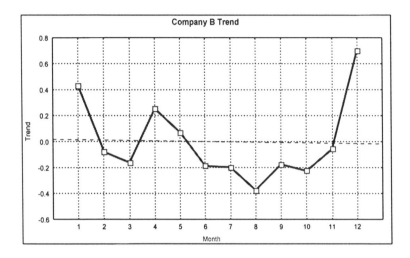

Chart 6. Company C is in manufacturing with 348 employees and 39 small and large team performance measures. The trend was not significant, but increased 1.25% per month.

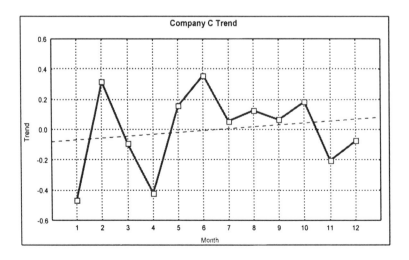

Chart 7. Company D is in banking with 464 employees and 18 large team performance measures. The trend was not significant but decreased -2.51% per month.

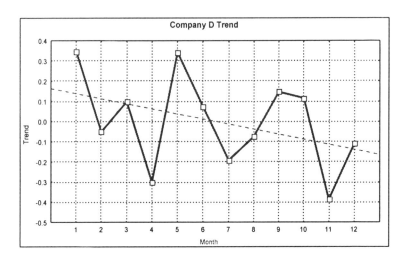

Chart 8. Company E is in publishing with 66 employees and 54 small team and individual performance measures. The trend was significant, and increased .15% per month.

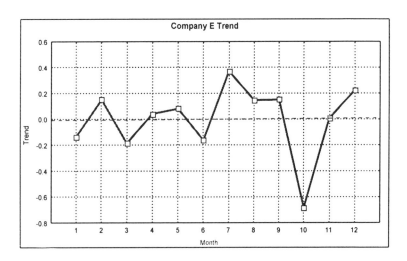

Chart 9. Company F is in distribution with 206 employees and 228 small team and individual performance measures. The trend was not significant, but decreased -.13% per month.

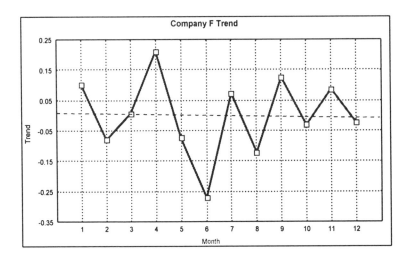

Chart 10. Company G is in retail banking with 747 employees and 536 small team and individual performance measures. The trend was significant and increased 3.83% per month.

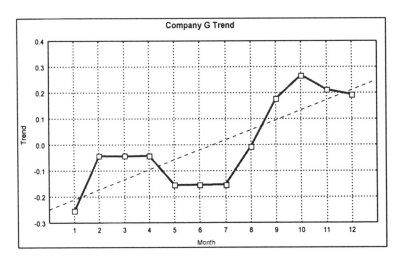

Chart 11. Company H is the operations area of Company G with 186 employees and 94 small team and individual performance measures. The trend was significant and increased 3.04% per month.

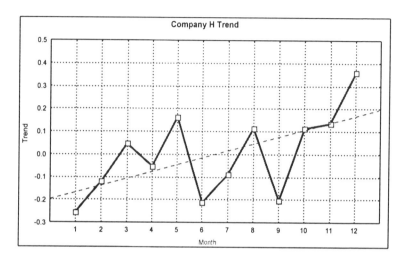

Chart 12. Company I is in distribution with 99 employees and 56 small team and individual performance measures. The trend was significant and decreased -1.06% per month.

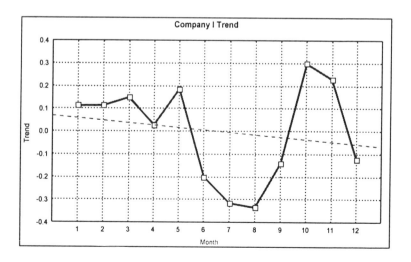

Chart 13. Company J is in banking with 1,140 employees and 618 small team and individual performance measures. The trend was not significant, but decreased -.11% per month.

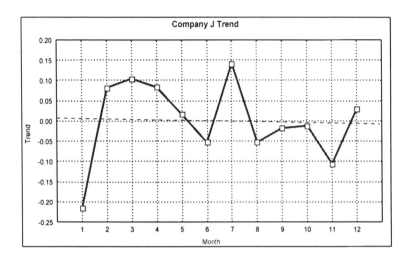

Chart 14. Company K is in distribution with 148 employees and 75 small team and individual performance measures. The trend was significant and increased 2.79% per month.

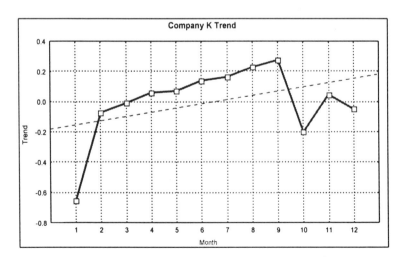

Chart 15. Company L is in manufacturing with 537 participating employees and 237 manager performance measures. The overall trend was significant and increased 2.56% per month.

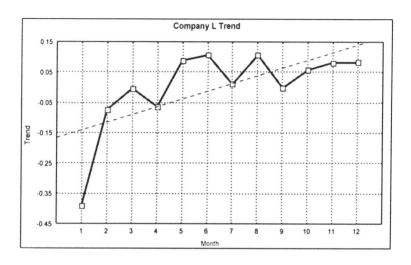

Analysis of Scorecard System Design Variables

1) Does performance improvement differ among the types of performance measures?

Measure Type Examples

Measure Type	Examples
Expense Control	cost / unit, percent budget met, expense / revenue
Sales	revenue, gross margin, cross-sell,
Quality	Quality measures refers to internal quality and include internal customer satisfaction ratings, % on-time, % accurate, quality checklists
Regulatory Compliance	safety, housekeeping and environmental checklists, recordable accidents, audits
Productivity	labor expense / unit, units / labor hour
Projects	% project milestones met, % days early/late, milestone quality rating
Customer Service	Customer service refers to external quality and includes customer satisfaction ratings, % on-time, % accurate, returns, account attrition

Table 4 and Chart 16 display average trends for each measure type. An analysis of variance finds a significant (p= .0012) difference between the measure type means.

Table 4

Measure Type	Trend	Standard Deviation	Number of Measures
Expense Control	.0075	.1357	326
Sales	.0058	.1218	581
Quality	.0255	.1120	513
Regulatory Comp	.0456	.1354	82
Productivity	.0094	.1220	463
Projects	.0128	.1250	64
Customer Service	.0413	.1180	166
All	.0158	.1226	2,195

Chart 16

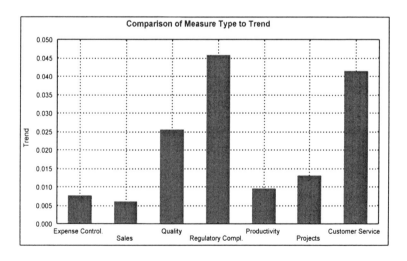

Quality, regulatory compliance and customer service measures improved more than other types of measures. A possible explanation is that employees have more 'discretionary control' over these types of measures than others. Employees have more direct influence on safe practices, on-time performance, and accuracy. Expense control and productivity (staffing levels) are more under the control of management than workers, although workers can create a productivity improvement opportunity through gains in efficiency and utilization. The modest gains in sales may be because sales feedback and commission plans were already in place in most cases. Project performance should have had higher gains if employee control is the underlying determinant. A possible explanation is that milestone setting behavior affects gains as much as actual project behavior. Since formal project tracking was new to all clients, this may account for these results.

2) Do team or individual scorecards yield the most performance improvement?

The 1,831 team measures' mean trend was .014 with a standard deviation of .1239. The 364 individual measures' mean was .023 with a standard deviation of .1160. A t-test for independent samples yielded a p = .214 indicating no significant difference in the effects of team vs. individual measures. This lack of significance may be due, in part, to unbalanced group sizes. Chart 17 compares the trends.

Chart 17

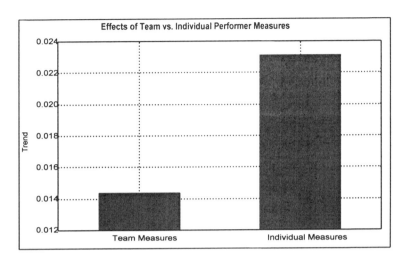

Team vs. Individual measures is viewed by measure type in chart 18. The data suggest that team measures yield better results for measure types where the team leader or manager has more discretionary control than the workers do.

Chart 18

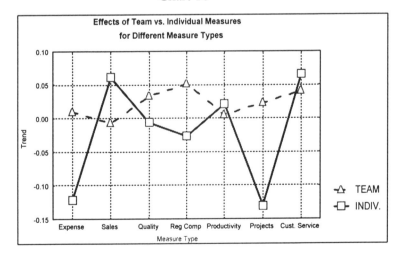

3) Do hourly employees respond more to the system than salaried employees?

The 1,210 salaried employee measures were compared to the 985 hourly employee measures. The salaried mean was .0036 with a standard deviation of .1186. The hourly employee mean was .0307 with a standard deviation of .1259. A t-test for independent samples yielded a significant p = .0000. Chart 19 displays the results.

Chart 19

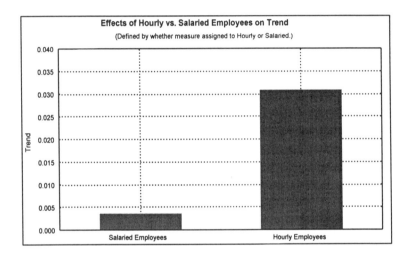

When the measure type in Chart 20 is considered, it appears that hourly employees perform better on all types except expense control and customer service. The lack of differences in expense control and customer service are likely due to these measures representing teams in which both managers and workers participate.

Chart 20

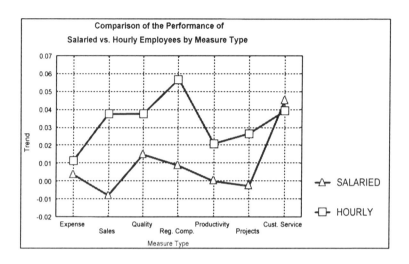

4) Does the complexity (employees per scorecard) of the system constrain performance improvements?

System complexity is computed as the number of employees divided by the number of scorecards. The most complex scorecard system will have one unique scorecard for each employee. The mean employees per scorecard across all companies was 2.24 with a standard deviation of 4.13. An F-test across values yielded a $p = .143$ which was not significant. Chart 21 displays the results. Performance trend remains consistent for up to twelve employees per scorecard after which trend decreases and variability increases. This suggests that trends improve in scorecards as the complexity decreases to a point at which the scorecards are too general and trends begin to decline.

Chart 21

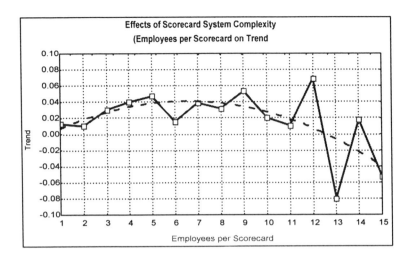

Note: x-axis displays employees per scorecard

5) Does the complexity of the individual scorecards (measures per scorecard) constrain performance improvements?

Scorecard complexity is computed by dividing the number of performance measures by the number of scorecards. The ratio is considered to be an indicator of the complexity of an organization's individual scorecards with the simplest scorecard having only one measure. The mean of this indicator was 5.04 with a standard deviation of 1.48. The minimum scorecard measure average was 1.00 while the maximum was 10.33. An F-test yielded a significant p = .016. Chart 22 displays the results.

Chart 22

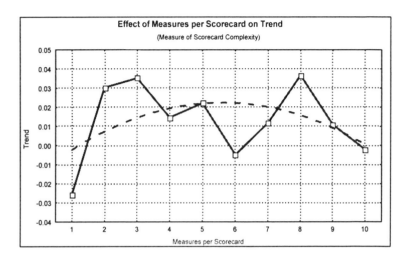

It is common to find more measures at higher organizational levels due to increased span of control and accountabilities. Chart 23 displays the effects of measures per scorecard on trend for salaried (managers) vs. hourly employees. These results find that increasing the number of scorecard measures has different effects on these two groups. The reasons are not clear.

Chart 23

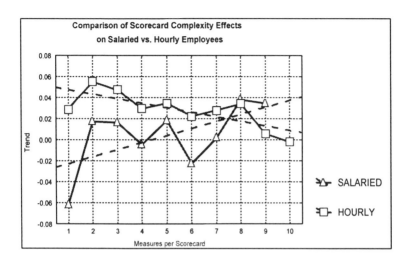

6) Does the priority weight assigned to a measure affect performance improvement?

A measure's priority weight can range from 0% to 100%. The weight determines both the measure's relative contribution to the scorecard's overall performance index and the incentive payout. The mean weight was 22.84% with a standard deviation of 14.50%. Weights ranged from 0 to 100%. The F-test yielded a significant effect with p = .00065. The fact that the mean weight is around 23% and the average measures per scorecard is about five indicates, that across all scorecards, measures tended to be evenly weighted. Chart 24 displays the results. A review of the chart finds rather nominal effects on trend until the weight exceeds 40%. Weights larger than 40% appear to drive increased variability in trend improvements. This may, in part, be due to changes in job types toward sales and production.

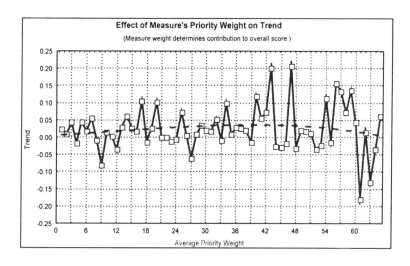

7) Does the level at which a measure's base or goal is set affect performance improvement?

The scorecard score is computed as a percent gain where percent gain = (actual − base) / (goal −base). All of the scorecards in the study interpolate this value on an eleven-point scale that typically ranges from −20% to 100%. All scorecards also have a partially accelerating scale in which the last two intervals are larger. This feature increases payouts as performance nears goal.

Typical Scorecard Scale

−20 −10 0 10 20 30 40 50 60 80 100

The percent gain formula is applied to the raw performance data and the result is assigned the scale interval it falls in (all values are rounded down). Scorecard scores are, of course, affected by actual performance data, but also by changes in the measure's base and/or goal. The mean score was 56.92 with a standard deviation of 35.94. Therefore, two-thirds of the scores fell between 19 and 93. The F-test was not significant with p = .083. Chart 25 displays the results. A review of the chart finds the variability in trends increases substantially as scores fall below 30 or exceed 135. Low scores affect both social and cash reinforcement while scores above 100% have no added value since, in most cases, the scale is capped at 100%.

Chart 25

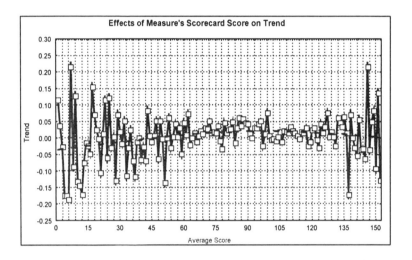

Effect of Scorecard Performance Index on Trend

The performance index is the sum of the weighted scores on a scorecard. In most cases, the PI can range from 0% to 100%. The index determines how much of an available incentive opportunity the employee earns. For example, if an employee were eligible for 10% of his base pay, and received a PI of 70%, the employee would earn 10% x 70% or 7% of his base pay. The mean performance index was 45.89 with a standard deviation of 23.4. Therefore, two-thirds of the PI's fell between 22 and 69. The indicator's F-test was significant with p = .016. A review of chart 26 finds a similar effect as the scores with trend variability increasing below about 20 and above 65. The effects of low and high PI's are the same as scores with the exception that the PI is the summary, and so directly affects social recognition and pay where individual scores can be offset by performances on other scorecard measures.

Chart 26

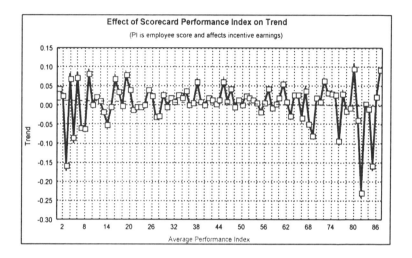

8) Do frequent changes in a measure's base, goal or weight affect performance improvement?

Scorecard measure parameters include the measure's base, goal, and priority weight. All measure definitions remained consistent over the study. The indicator 'changes' is the number of times a parameter was changed in the twelve-month period. The mean and standard deviation for base changes was .285 and .729; for goal changes .278 and .636; and for weights .272 and .491. The similarity in these means and standard deviations suggests that often two or more parameter changes were performed simultaneously (most likely base and goal). The F-tests for the effect of each change on trend were base = p = .070, goal = p = .141, and weight = p =.293. Though none are significant, base and goal changes appear to be more important than weight changes.

Charts 27, 28, and 29 display the results. Changes in any one of the parameters appear to lower the performance trend.

Chart 27: Changes to the Base

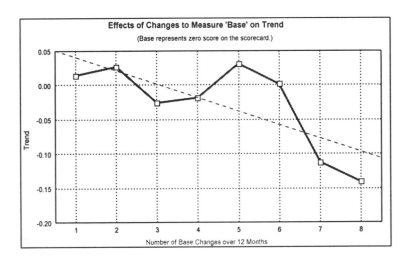

Chart 28: Changes to the Goal

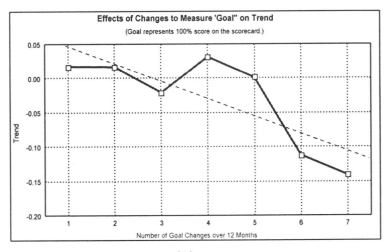

Chart 29: Changes to the Weight

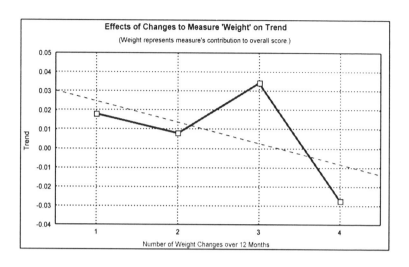

Analysis of Incentive Pay Variables

9) Does the level of incentive pay opportunity affect performance trend?

Effect of Guaranteed Incentive Opportunity on Performance Trend.

A guaranteed incentive opportunity is the same each month for an entire year and is not adjusted for company profitability or any other factors. Opportunity represents the most an employee can potentially earn. Opportunity is multiplied by the employee's scorecard performance to determine the actual incentive payout. Table 5 categorizes the measure counts for various levels of guaranteed incentive opportunity.

Table 5

Incentive Opportunity %	Measure Count	Percent of Total
0%	1,020	46.44%
0% – 10%	1,000	45.61%
11% – 20%	137	6.24%
21% – 30%	21	.94%
31% – 40%	2	.09%
41% – 50%	15	.68%
Average = 4.58%		
Std Dev = 6.03%, Max = 46%		100.00%

Chart 30 compares guaranteed opportunity to trend. A negative exponential trend line best fits the data. There is an unexpected absence of any significant relationship between the level of guaranteed incentive opportunity and performance trend.

Chart 30

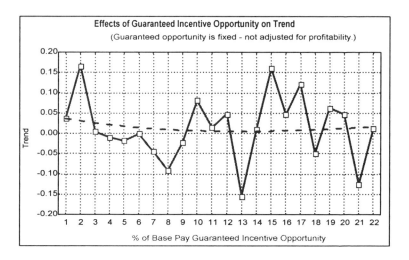

Effects of Total Incentive Opportunity on Performance Trend

Total incentive opportunity includes both guaranteed opportunity and profit-indexed opportunity. Profit-indexed opportunity varies each month depending on the profitability of the organization. Total opportunity is multiplied by the employee's scorecard performance to determine the actual incentive payout.

Table 6 on the following page categorizes the measure counts for various levels of total incentive opportunity.

Table 6

Incentive Opportunity %	Measure Count	Percent of Total
0%	470	21.41%
0% – 10%	865	39.41%
11% – 20%	744	33.90%
21% – 30%	76	3.46%
31% – 40%	21	.96%
41% –50%	4	.18%
51% –60%	9	.41%
61 –70%	0	0.00%
71 –80%	6	.27%
Average = 9.57%		

Chart 31 compares average total incentive opportunity to performance trend. A negative exponential trend line shows that as opportunity increases above 29% of base pay, the performance trend increases. One interpretation of the results of chart 30 and 31 is that incentive pay opportunity must be 30% or higher to influence performance.

Chart 31

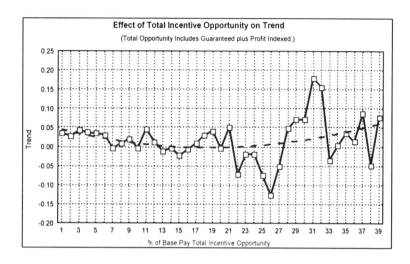

10) Does the level of incentive payout affect performance trend?

Incentive payout is computed as the employee's scorecard performance index multiplied by both guaranteed opportunity and profit-indexed opportunity for the month. The payout represents what the employee earns as a percentage of her base pay. Table 7 categorizes the measure counts for various levels of average incentive payout.

Table 7

Incentive Payout %	Measure Count	Percent of Total
0%	470	21.41%
0% – 10%	1386	63.14%

11% – 20%	293	13.36%
21% –30%	27	1.23%
31% – 40%	11	.50%
41% –50%	6	.36%
Average = 5.44%		
Std Dev = 5.54%, Max = 45%		100.00%

Chart 32 compares average incentive payout percentage to trend. A negative exponential trend shows that the level of payout affects performance trend. Where opportunity improved performance above 30%, an actual payout percentage of 20% or higher appeared to improve performance.

Chart 32

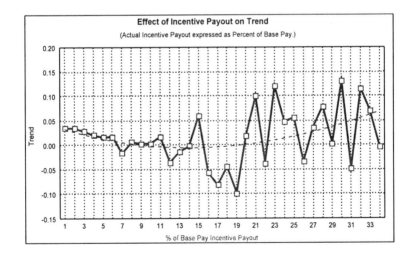

Discussion

A cluster analysis was performed to determine if the structural variables could be logically grouped. Three groups were identified.

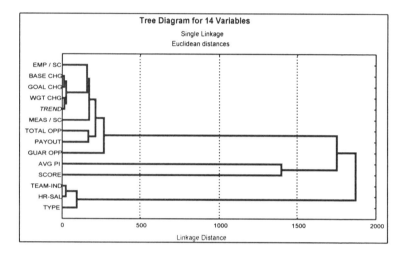

Group I: Scorecard Design and Administrative Variables. The above cluster analysis roughly generates three clusters of interest. The first cluster includes employees / scorecard, base changes, goal changes, weight changes and measures per scorecard. These variables are considered 'scorecard design and administrative' variables.

Group II: Incentive Pay Variables. The second cluster includes incentive payout, total incentive opportunity, incentive payout, guaranteed incentive opportunity, average performance index, and average score. These variables are considered the 'incentive pay' variables.

Group III: Organizational Structure Variables. The third cluster includes team vs. individual measures, hourly vs. salaried, and measure type. These variables are considered the 'organizational structure' variables because the nature of the business determines, in part, whether measures can be defined for individuals, the hourly – salaried mix, and the type of measures employed.

Group I: Scorecard Design and Administrative Recommendations. The first three issues (1-3) compared performance trend to measure types, team vs. individual measures, and hourly vs. salaried employees. The general finding was that the more 'discretionary control' employees have over a measure – the greater the performance improvement. This finding supports the view that individual and small team measures are more effective at prompting and reinforcing performance improvement than are larger group measures. Care should be taken in the development of the measurement system to ensure that participants can directly influence the measures selected.

The next two issues (4-5) explored the relationship of scorecard system complexity and individual scorecard measure complexity to performance trends. Complex systems should increase performance trends to warrant the increased administration and communication such systems require. The results of these analyses suggest an 'optimal' system complexity of from three to twelve employees per scorecard. Performance trends tend to decline above or below this range. The optimal number of measures per scorecard are not clear, but the results do tentatively suggest that hourly employees may be more sensitive to high numbers of scorecard measures than salaried employees.

The next two issues (6–7) explored the relationship of specific measure parameters to performance trends. These parameters included the measure's priority weight, base and goal, and the overall scorecard performance index achieved by the employees. A measure's priority weight appears to have little effect on performance until it is defined at 40% or more. At these levels, the variability in trend across weightings increases but there is no clear relationship to performance trend. This may be due to the confounding effect that high priority weights tend to be applied to more one-dimensional jobs like sales and production.

Similarly, a measure's base levels, goal levels, and scorecard performance indexes do not present simple, linear relationships to performance trend. The variability in trend across the average measure score increases below 30 and above 135. Performance trend variability also increases when the scorecard's performance index falls outside a range of from about 20 to 65. These results suggest that more consistent performance improvement is achieved when bases and goals are assigned that produce scores that fall in the middle range of the scorecard scale. This may be due to low scores creating adverse social and monetary outcomes while scores above one hundred percent do not increase incentive payouts because they are 'capped.' Further, scores well above one-hundred percent encourage management to increase the goal requirements.

The next issue (8) concerns scorecard administration. Does performance improve more when bases, goals and weights are consistently changed, or when these parameters remain relatively constant? The findings support the latter view for all three scorecard parameters – especially bases and goals. The recommendation is to minimize the number of base and goal changes throughout the year.

Group II: Incentive Pay Recommendations. Issues 9 – 10 explored the relationship between incentive opportunity and payout to performance trend. Though not a strong effect, it appears that the levels of both incentive opportunity and payout affect performance trends. However, this relationship is not linear. Payout effects on performance trend appear at around 20% of base pay while opportunity effects appear at around 30% of base pay. Incentive pay can be expensive and often reduces the performance system's flexibility with respect to parameter changes. Organizations considering incentive pay should only do so if the incentive opportunity will be substantial. Given this, the practice of indexing incentive pay opportunity to profitability is critical. Indexing incentive opportunity to profit ensures the 'affordability' of the incentives and ensures the organization remains competitive.

Group III: Organizational Structure Recommendations. The findings indicate that organizations that are able to define and track measures that are 'close to the individual', and that provide employee's some discretion in how they achieve the goal, will experience greater performance improvement than organization's that either must, or choose to, measure high level group indicators. There is little evidence that incentive pay opportunity or incentive payouts influence performance improvement unless these conditions are first met. If not, incentive pay may be a poor investment. Organizations considering a performance improvement initiative should also include hourly employees, since this group experienced the most performance improvement.

Conclusions

The average trend improvement for all twelve companies was 2.76% a month or 33.12% annually. Six of the companies achieved statistically significant trends that averaged .0276%. These companies' employee groups ranged from 54 employees to 536 and represented industries including manufacturing, retail, publishing, distribution, and banking. The combination of performance scorecards and incentive pay had a positive effect on employee performance in eight diverse companies.

Average client improvement (33%) with an average 7% payout

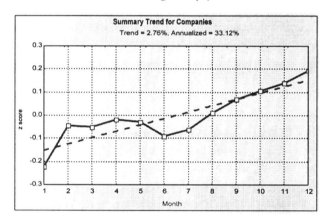

The most important variable examined was the level of control employees had over their assigned performance measures. Individual measures produced more improvement than team measures, hourly employees improved more than salaried, more controllable measure types displayed more improvement, and a low number of changes in scorecard parameters increased improvement.

Surprisingly, only high levels of incentive pay appeared to have a relationship to performance improvement. The relationship of measure controllability and incentive magnitude may be roughly analogous to Newton's general gravity principle. The closer a measure is to an employee's personal control, the more the measure "attracts" the employee's interest. As the measure moves away from personal control, the incentive pay magnitude (and other consequences) required to produce an equivalent improvement must increase substantially.

Unfortunately, it is often impractical to measure critical organizational outcomes at the personal control level. In these cases, "performance management" is required to bring the measure closer to the individual. Managers can bridge the gap by pinpointing employee behaviors and outcomes that directly relate to scorecard measures. Managers can further enhance employee control through prompting, timely feedback, and working with employees to develop behavioral and process improvement plans. This assertion is confirmed by the fact that only one organization in the study (company L) did not provide an incentive pay opportunity for its employees yet had the third highest overall improvement. Company L implemented significant process improvement and performance training for its managers prior to the introduction of the scorecard system. No other company in the study provided its managers these skills.

The authors have chosen to begin their analysis of these data with an examination of 'large' effects across a diverse population. Future studies will look at more specific relationships including specific measure types (accuracy, timeliness, customer surveys, efficiency, utilization, prospecting, closing, etc.). A more detailed examination of the conditions under which incentive pay works best is underway as well as an investigation of performance management issues including feedback, manager behavior, and performance improvement planning activities.

Chapter 20

Managing Without Supervising

Section I provided an overview of the problems with conventional management and pay practices and proposed an alternative Total Performance System. Section II described how performance measures and scorecards are designed. Section III explained how performance pay could be linked to both employee scorecard performance and organizational profitability. Section IV concluded with recommendations for the on-going management of a Total Performance System.

The components of an effective performance system are a combination of team and personal scorecard measures, automated monthly reporting, team meetings, diagnostic trend data, and tactical improvement planning. The system is sustained through stakeholder pay in which a portion of base pay is exchanged for a higher incentive pay opportunity linked to profitability and scorecard performance.

The ultimate question that must occur to the reader is – "Is it worth it?" Business organizations have operated with conventional direct supervision for hundreds of years. Why change? There are, in fact, both pragmatic and organizational cultural reasons for considering a change to a self-regulated performance system.

Pragmatic Reasons for a Transition to a Self-Regulating Performance System

1. Technology. The conventional management system came into its own in the 1940's. Wages and salaries replaced piece-rates and annual pay increases were awarded to reflect an ever-increasing cost of living. Direct supervision gradually replaced the piece-rate as a management strategy.

Though there were several reasons for this change in management practices, two that have increasingly fueled the transition are the increased complexity and variability of job requirements and the transition to a 'service' society. These events made it increasingly more difficult to efficiently measure employee performances.

Two technologies have evolved to the point that it is now practical to consider returning to direct measurement and performance pay. Innovations in data gathering and data processing now allow for efficient direct measurement of complex performance systems. Second, the field of applied behavior analysis provides the concepts and practices necessary for the management of complex performance systems.

2. **Decentralization.** Direct supervision requires direct observation and contact with subordinates. Direct contact is often impractical in many of today's organizations where employees work at home, in remote locations, or consistently travel. Performance measurement and incentive pay offer a practical alternative.

3. **Consolidation.** Over the past several years, organizations have been growing through acquisition and strategic alliances. The resulting organizations may lack any shared supervisory culture or practices. A Total Performance System would efficiently align supervisors and teams with the new organization's strategy and tactics.

4. **Employee diversity.** Today's employee comes from a variety of cultures that make it increasingly difficult for the traditional supervisor to function effectively in command and control. Direct measures help reduce the impact of cultural differences.

5. **Employee turnover.** Today's employee is less likely to commit to an organization and sees himself as a 'free agent'. Creating a partnership with these employees through stakeholder pay, makes it more likely they will commit to the long-term.

6. Supervision expense. Increased competition squeezes profit margins. Direct measurement and incentive pay enable managers to increase their span of control and thus significantly reduce overall supervision expense.

7. Customer focus. Conventional management and pay has severed the critical relationship between employees and customers. The Total Performance System reestablishes the link between paying customers and employee earnings. The result is a greater focus on customer needs.

Organizational Cultural Reasons for a Transition to a Self-Regulating Performance System.

1. Self-reliance. The American culture's success resulted, in large part, from the kind of people who immigrated here. These immigrants were risk-takers and self-reliant. We have lost these characteristics as the society has matured, and are beginning to suffer for it. The organization that can rekindle this spirit will benefit in the same ways the society did during its development.

2. Entitlement Thinking. Many people have come to believe they are entitled to a good job and a good living without regard for their personal contribution to the organization's success. They assume the company has infinite resources and owes them a living. The connection between effort and reward has been severed.

3. Entrepreneurship. The entrepreneur has been the source of this country's innovation and growth. Today, this is apparent in the thousands of high-tech and dot.com start-up companies. Many of these entrepreneurs left established organizations to start their own businesses or join start-up companies. The organizations they leave are losing their most important resources.

Traditional management and pay practices discourage and even punish innovation and initiative. The Total Performance System offers the entrepreneur the opportunity to be 'self-employed' within an organization through recognizing personal contribution and sharing profits.

4. Class warfare. It is commonly accepted that there must be an adversarial relationship among ownership, management, and workers. Owners feel managers and workers want too much and produce too little. Managers feel owners have unreasonable expectations and workers are unproductive. Workers feel that owners and managers are getting rich at their expense.

These conflicts largely stem from conventional management and pay practices. Ownership and management do not share information with employees because they feel they have no need or right to the information since their pay is guaranteed. When the company does well, managers and workers usually do not personally share in the success. On the other hand, when the company performs poorly, ownership takes all the risks (at least until layoffs occur).

The answer is to create a genuine partnership among owners, managers, and workers. A partnership in which personal and team accomplishments are directly and meaningfully, rewarded. A partnership in which every contributor shares in profit gains.

5. Expanded Opportunity. In my consulting with organizations, I frequently hear managers argue that strategic alignment and stakeholder pay may make sense for managers, but will not be well received or understood by low level workers.

In fact, the opposite is often true. Conventional pay is a 'commodity' system in which education, experience, and local job market pay practices determine an employee's value (salary) to the organization. In contrast, stakeholder pay indexes pay to performance and the organization's profitability. Therefore, employees with little education or experience will fare better under stakeholder pay then they will under conventional pay.

For example, if I seek a job I will present my education and job experiences to potential employers. These, and a few other factors, will establish my price or value. However, I am actually self-employed. What, then, is my 'market value'. The question, of course, makes no sense. I earn whatever customers are willing to pay me, adjusted for how well I control my expenses. That is, I earn as much as I am able to produce.

In a stakeholder pay organization, the same principles apply. The worker earns as much as her performance and the organization's profitability provide. Her earnings are tied to her performance rather than her job and educational history. Employees with the least education and experience have the most to gain from stakeholder pay–and they know it. That is why I have most often first received approval from the worker ranks.

6. Transition from Negative to Positive Reinforcement.

The psychologist, B.F. Skinner, developed reinforcement theory. Unfortunately, the theory has been widely misunderstood. Because reinforcement theory helps a great deal in understanding the impact of organizational practices on employee behavior, the theory will be briefly explained.

Skinner's theory is that the probability we will engage in a behavior is influenced by its consequences. If the consequences of doing something are beneficial, we will likely do it again. If there are no consequences, or adverse consequences, we are less likely to do it again. In other words, through interacting with our surroundings, we learn which behaviors benefit us and which behaviors don't. Skinner termed consequences that make us more likely to do something again, reinforcers, and the process reinforcement.

There are two broad classes of reinforcers. Those that increase the probability of a behavior through their application, and those that increase the probability of a behavior through their removal or avoidance. For example, if I help my wife store the groceries and she then comments on how helpful I am, I am more likely to help her again. This relationship is termed positive reinforcement. On the other hand, I could fail to help her and she might criticize me for being no help. To avoid the criticism in the future, I would help her out the next time. This relationship is termed negative reinforcement. In both cases, the likelihood that I will help out in the future has been increased.

Unfortunately, a good deal of what we do is driven more so by negative reinforcement than positive. A lot of our time is spent avoiding unpleasant outcomes rather than seeking out beneficial ones. Avoidance behavior is especially problematic because it is difficult to unlearn. The old joke goes: "A man is standing on a street corner in the middle of town waving his arms frantically. A passerby asks him why he's waving his arms. He replies it is to keep the elephants away. The passerby explains that there are no elephants. The response is, see it works!"

Most managers and supervisors rely partly or completely on negative reinforcement to maintain subordinate performance. The annual performance review is more likely negative reinforcement than positive. Many employees work during the year to avoid a bad review. After a good review, they feel more relieved than rewarded.

Though negative reinforcement does maintain the target behavior, it carries with it a good deal of undesirable baggage. People tend to perform only to minimum expectations. The reason is simple. There is no benefit to performance above minimum requirements, and the real possibility exists that the standard (and fear) will be increased if performance exceeds the minimum.

Negative reinforcement prompts 'escape' behaviors including poor attendance and turnover. Negative reinforcement generates apprehension, which may reduce employee effectiveness–particularly in complex or customer-related tasks. However, the most profound impact of negative reinforcement is that it dramatically reduces employee initiative and creativity. In a fear-driven workplace, the employee is loath to try something new for fear of adverse consequences.

7. Back to our roots. The free enterprise system has consistently outperformed socialism and communism in both innovation and wealth generation. The failures of central planning and bureaucracy are well known, and yet we continue to apply these approaches within our organizations. Why, then, is corporate socialism the norm? The answer is not particularly flattering. Wages and salaries, management by exception, and subjective management are simply more familiar and easier to apply. The problem is not bad management – the problem is lazy management.

A sad commentary is that many highly successful entrepreneurs create organizations in which they would never work. The freedom and direct rewards provided by a free economy are what spawned their entrepreneurial behavior, but they do not provide a similar environment for their own employees.

The tools needed to create such an organization have been outlined in this book and have proven successful in a diverse collection of organizations. It is time to strip away the outmoded management practices of the 40's and to create self-regulating performance systems that empower employees and meaningfully recognize their contributions to the success of the organization.

References

p. 15.	Laurence J. Peter and Raymond Hull. *The Peter Principle.* New York: William Morrow & Co., 1978.
p. 15	William H. Whyte, Jr. *The Organization Man.* New York: Doubleday & Co., 1957.
pp. 20-27	William B. Abernathy. *The Sin of Wages.* Memphis, TN: PerfSys Press, 1996.
p. 48	B.F. Skinner. *Walden Two.* New York: Prentice-Hall, 1976.
pp. 49, 98	G.H. Felix and J.L. Riggs. *Productivity by the Objectives Matrix.* Corvalis, OR: Oregon Productivity Center, 1986.
p. 55	Thomas F. Gilbert. *Human Competence: Engineering Worthy Performance.* New York: McGraw-Hill, 1978.
pp. 57, 277	Robert S. Kaplan and David P. Norton. *The Balanced Scorecard: Translating Strategy into Action.* Cambridge, MA: Harvard Business School Publishing, 1996.
p. 203	Martin Weitzman. *The Share Economy.* Cambridge, MA: Harvard University Press, 1984.
p. 327	B.F. Skinner. *Contingencies of Reinforcement: A Theoretical Analysis.* New York: Appleton-Century-Croft, 1969.

Index

A
management practices survey, 38
tactical improvement plan, 229
accelerating intervals, 105
activity vs. outcome, 51
administration obstacles, 293
administrative checklist, 179
administrative procedures, 281
alternative conversion scales, 105
alternative pay systems, 188
antecedents & consequences, 224
Applied Behavior Analysis, 8

B
base and goal, 108
base or goal, 248
base pay, 196
basis, 197
behavior consequences, 257
Behavior Contingency Analysis and Observation Guide, 261
behavior contingency issues, 259
behavior feedback, 256
behavior or process measures, 53
behavior prompts, 256
behaviorists, 8
bonus plans, 224
bookkeeping performance measure, 181
bottom-up: piece-meal measurement and incentive pay implementations, 56
bottom-up: system process measurement and incentive pay implementations, 57
budgeted incentive opportunity, 199
budgets, 156
bureaucratic management, 10

C
cascading objectives, 33
Case Study, 61
cash flow, 91
cash flow formula, 147
change effort, 16
close ratio, 132
collections, 147
commission and piece-rate, 190, 192
commodity labor thinking, 19, 30
comparison of different plans' effectiveness, 191
component analysis, 262
composite measures, 124
consolidated multi-dimensional performance measurement, 48
controllability, 248
conventional management, 31
conventional pay, 195, 209
conversion scale with Stretch intervals, 106
corporate socialism, 24
cross-sell ratio, 132
cross-utilization, 143
customer satisfaction, 7, 92
customer service, 157
customer service surveys, 167

D
decentralization, 6, 339

diagnostic measures, 103

E
efficiency,140 142
employee diversity, 339
employee empowerment, 55, 126
employee involvement, 57
employee risk-taking factors, 214
employee turnover, 339
entitlement pay, 5,22
entitlement thinking, 19, 27, 340
entrepreneurship, 340
existing bonus plans, 207
expense control, 91,155
external equity, 275

F
feedback, 229
fixed-cost pay, 21
flow ratio, 147
focus, 248
framing effect, 272
free market, 13
frequency of feedback, 115

G
gainsharing, 191, 193
goal setting, 109,111
goal sharing, 190, 192
group plans, 290
group size, 121
guaranteed incentive opportunity, 325

H
high performer retention, 280

I
implementation obstacles, 291
incentive opportunity, 326
incentive pay objectives, 188
incentive pay recommendations, 334
incentive payout, 329
inside sales, 136
internal equity, 275
inventory control, 149

L
leadership analysis, 276
leverage, 274
Lincoln Electric, 5, 13
linear conversion scale, 106
linked measures, 128
linked sales measures, 133
locus of control, 17

M
management by perception, 26
management styles, 225
management through fear, 232. 235
manager success factors, 283
managing through positive reinforcement, 238
measure validity, 248
multiplier, 197
multiplier scale design, 202
multiplier scale threshold, 203

N
negative reinforcement, 17, 232 343
net productivity, 141

O
obstacles to implementation, 13, 287
one-dimensional performance measurement, 42
opportunity adjusted measures, 52
opportunity adjustments, 127

organizational cultural reasons for a transition to a self-regulating performance system, 340
organizational structure tecommendations, 334
outside sales, 130

P
pay for time, 23
payables measures, 151
payout delay, 273
payout frequency, 202
payroll and benefits manager/staff, 186
percent gain, 101
performance analysis, 239
performance charts, 35
performance improvement issues, 255
performance index, 269
performance management, 222
performance matrix, 100
performance measurement categories, 90
performance opportunity adjustment, 124
performance pay analysis, 270
performance pay return, 276
performance pay system audit measures, 270
performance points, 49
performance review, 121
performance scales, 112
performance scorecard, 34, 100
performance scorecard analysis, 266
performance system administrative structures, 280
performance system analysis, 244
performance system procedures and policies, 284
performance trend, 279
performance variability, 279
performance-based promotions, 25
Peter Principle, 25
piece rate, 43
Positive Leadership, 38, 222
positive reinforcement, 17, 343
pragmatic reasons for a transition to a self-regulating performance system, 338
priority weights, 98, 107
process analysis, 243
process issues, 262
production team scorecards, 144
productivity, 91, 140
profit center determined incentive opportunity, 200
profit sharing, 191, 193
profit-indexed pay increases, 217
profit-indexed performance pay, 40, 191, 193, 196
programming measures, 176
project measures, 172
prospecting, 131
purchasing manager/staff, 151

R
recruiter performance, 182
regulatory compliance, 92, 171
result vs. process measures, 116
rework, 140
risk-taking factors, 214

S
safety, 171
sales, 91
sales credits, 130
sales measure, 130
sales ratio, 132
sales/selling hour, 131
scale end-points, 103

scale intervals, 104
scorecard revision policies, 283
scorecard system blueprint, 96
scorecard system audit measures, 266
scorecard validity, 282
selection or training, 256
self-regulated performance system, 338
service and product quality, 163
service response timeliness, 158
service style, 164
service surveys, 167
service/product deadline, 161
service/product turnaround, 160
share percentage, 204
situational analysis, 245
stakeholder pay, 211, 219
standard time, 48
strategic scorecard, 32, 89
strategy-based measurement Implementations, 58
subjective management, 15
subjective measures, 120
sub-scorecards, 102
supervision expense, 340
support position measures, 178, 180
system review, 39
systems perspectives, 8

T
tactical analysis, 240
tactical improvement plan, 37
Ten Commandments of performance measurement, 114
therapeutic model, 9
threshold, 198
Total Performance System, 5, 28, 29, 89

trainer performance measures, 184
transition from negative to positive reinforcement, 342
transition strategies, 217

U
unconsolidated, multi-dimensional measurement plans, 47
utilization, 140

V
vertical-sell ratio, 132

W
Walden Two, 50
warehouse manager/staff, 153
weighted score, 112

Notes

Notes

Notes

Notes